I0003640

THE DOUBLE SIDES OF TECHNOLOGY

INTERNET ADDICTION AND ITS IMPACT ON TODAY'S SOCIETY

DAVID SANDUA

The Double Sides of Technology.

© David Sandua 2024. All rights reserved.

eBook & Paperback Edition.

"The internet has become such a part of our lives that it is easy to overlook how profoundly it is changing us."

Clay Shirky

ÍNDEX

I. INTRODUCTION

The advent of the internet has revolutionized the way we communicate, work, and access information. However, along with its many benefits, the internet has brought about a new concern: internet addiction. Defined as a behavioral disorder characterized by excessive internet use that interferes with daily life, internet addiction has become a growing issue in today's society. With the increasing prevalence of smartphones, social media platforms, and online gaming, individuals of all ages are at risk of developing problematic internet usage habits. This phenomenon raises important questions about the psychological and social implications of technology dependence. Understanding the factors that contribute to internet addiction and its impact on individuals' well-being is crucial for developing effective prevention and intervention strategies. In this research, we will explore the double sides of technology, examining the prevalence, causes, and consequences of internet addiction in contemporary society.

DEFINITION OF INTERNET ADDICTION

The concept of Internet addiction has been a topic of discussion and research for several years, with varying definitions proposed by scholars in the field. Internet addiction, also known as problematic internet use or compulsive internet use, is generally characterized by an individual's excessive and uncontrollable use of the internet, leading to negative consequences in their daily life. It is often associated with a loss of control, preoccupation with online activities, withdrawal symptoms when not online, and continued use despite negative outcomes. While the exact definition may differ slightly depending on the research perspective, most definitions encompass the idea that internet addiction can have significant detrimental effects on an individual's mental health, relationships, work or academic performance, and overall well-being. As society becomes increasingly reliant on technology, understanding and addressing internet addiction is crucial for promoting healthy and balanced use of the internet in today's interconnected world.

PREVALENCE OF INTERNET ADDICTION IN MODERN SOCIETY

The prevalence of internet addiction in modern society is a growing concern that has garnered increasing attention from researchers and mental health professionals. With the ubiquity of digital devices and widespread access to the internet, individuals are more susceptible to developing problematic usage patterns that can significantly impact their daily lives. Studies have shown that internet addiction is associated with various negative consequences, including poor academic performance, social withdrawal, and mental health issues. Furthermore, the continuous engagement with online activities can lead to a loss of control over internet use, resulting in detrimental effects on personal relationships and overall well-being. As technology continues to advance at a rapid pace, it is crucial to address the issue of internet addiction proactively through comprehensive interventions and public education initiatives to mitigate its detrimental effects on individuals and society as a whole.

PURPOSE AND STRUCTURE OF THE ESSAY

The purpose of this essay is to examine the double-sided nature of technology, specifically focusing on internet addiction and its impact on today's society. The structure of this essay will begin by defining internet addiction and providing an overview of its prevalence and consequences. Following this, the essay will delve into the factors that contribute to the development of internet addiction, such as individual vulnerabilities and environmental triggers. Next, the discussion will shift towards the societal implications of internet addiction, including its effects on mental health, relationships, and productivity. Furthermore, the essay will explore potential solutions and interventions to address internet addiction at both individual and societal levels. By critically evaluating the phenomenon of internet addiction and its multifaceted impact, this essay aims to provide a comprehensive analysis that contributes to the ongoing discourse on the intersection of technology and society.

II. HISTORICAL PERSPECTIVE OF INTERNET USAGE

The historical perspective of internet usage provides valuable insights into the evolution and impact of technology on society. From its humble beginnings in the 1960s as a tool for military communication to the widespread adoption in the 1990s as a global communication network, the internet has reshaped how individuals interact and access information. The rapid advancement of internet technologies has fueled unprecedented connectivity and accessibility, ushering in the age of digital transformation. However, along with the benefits, challenges such as internet addiction have emerged, raising concerns about its impact on societal well-being. Understanding the historical context of internet usage is crucial in navigating the complexities of technology's double-edged sword in today's society. By examining the historical trajectory of the internet, researchers can gain a deeper understanding of its influence on behavior, relationships, and mental health in the modern world.

EVOLUTION OF THE INTERNET

The evolution of the Internet has been a fascinating journey marked by significant technological advancements and societal implications. Beginning with the development of ARPANET in the 1960s, the Internet has grown exponentially, transforming the way we communicate, access information, and conduct business. The advent of the World Wide Web in the 1990s revolutionized the Internet, enabling users to navigate and interact with content on a global scale. As the Internet evolved, so did the challenges it brought, including issues of privacy, security, and digital divide. Today, with the rise of social media, e-commerce, and cloud computing, the Internet continues to shape our daily lives in ways we could not have imagined decades ago. Understanding the evolution of the Internet is crucial in analyzing its impact on society and addressing the potential risks and benefits associated with its use.

MILESTONES IN INTERNET ACCESSIBILITY

One of the significant milestones in internet accessibility was the introduction of the World Wide Web Consortium's Web Content Accessibility Guidelines (WCAG) in 1999. These guidelines set standards for web accessibility, ensuring that websites are usable for individuals with disabilities. Another milestone came with the passage of the Americans with Disabilities Act (ADA) in 1990, which mandated that public entities, including websites, must be accessible to individuals with disabilities. These milestones marked a shift towards a more inclusive online environment, where everyone, regardless of their abilities, could have equal access to information and services. As technology continues to advance, it is crucial to build upon these milestones and further improve internet accessibility to create a truly inclusive digital world. By implementing universal design principles and staying updated on accessibility guidelines, we can ensure that the internet remains a tool for empowerment and connectivity for all individuals.

SHIFTS IN SOCIETAL INTERACTION WITH TECHNOLOGY

The advancement of technology has led to significant shifts in societal interaction, particularly in the realm of communication and socialization. The proliferation of smartphones and social media platforms has transformed the way individuals connect and engage with one another, blurring the lines between virtual and physical interactions. As technology continues to evolve, people are increasingly reliant on digital communication channels for socializing, networking, and even forming relationships. This shift has raised concerns about the impact of excessive screen time on personal relationships and mental health, as individuals may prioritize virtual connections over face-to-face interactions. Furthermore, the rise of internet addiction and its associated consequences highlight the need for a critical examination of our changing relationship with technology. As society grapples with the implications of these shifts, it is imperative to consider how we can harness the benefits of technology while mitigating its potential drawbacks.

III. THE PSYCHOLOGY BEHIND INTERNET ADDICTION

The psychology behind internet addiction is a complex and multifaceted issue that involves various psychological factors. Individuals who become addicted to the internet often display symptoms similar to those seen in traditional substance addictions, such as withdrawal symptoms, tolerance, and difficulty controlling their use. Psychological theories suggest that internet addiction may be linked to underlying issues such as low self-esteem, loneliness, depression, or anxiety. In some cases, individuals may use the internet as a coping mechanism to escape from real-life problems or to fulfill unmet emotional needs. Additionally, the instant gratification and constant stimulation provided by the internet can create a cycle of reward and reinforcement that further fuels addictive behaviors. Understanding the psychological mechanisms driving internet addiction is essential for developing effective prevention and treatment strategies to address this growing societal concern.

COGNITIVE MECHANISMS OF ADDICTION

One of the key aspects to consider when examining internet addiction is the cognitive mechanisms that underlie this phenomenon. Addiction, whether it be substance-related or behavioral, often involves disruptions in cognitive processes such as reward processing, decision-making, and inhibitory control. In the context of internet addiction, individuals may exhibit heightened sensitivity to rewarding stimuli online, leading to compulsive behaviors and an inability to regulate their usage. Moreover, impaired decision-making abilities may contribute to excessive time spent online, as individuals may prioritize immediate gratification over long-term consequences. Additionally, deficits in inhibitory control can make it challenging for individuals to resist the urge to engage in online activities, further perpetuating their addictive behaviors. Understanding these cognitive mechanisms is crucial in developing effective interventions and strategies to address internet addiction and its impact on today's society. By targeting these cognitive processes, interventions can help individuals regain control over their online behaviors and reduce the negative consequences associated with excessive internet use.

EMOTIONAL TRIGGERS FOR ONLINE ENGAGEMENT

Emotional triggers play a crucial role in driving online engagement, shaping the behavior of individuals in the digital sphere. Understanding these triggers is essential for comprehending the complex relationship between individuals and technology. Research has shown that emotions such as fear, excitement, curiosity, and social validation can significantly impact online engagement levels. For instance, fear of missing out (FOMO) can drive individuals to constantly check their social media feeds, seeking validation and connection with others. On the other hand, feelings of excitement and curiosity can motivate individuals to explore new online platforms and content. Furthermore, the desire for social validation and acceptance can lead individuals to engage in excessive online activities in search of approval from their digital peers. By delving into the emotional triggers that influence online engagement, we can gain valuable insights into the mechanisms behind internet addiction and its implications for society.

BEHAVIORAL PATTERNS ASSOCIATED WITH INTERNET OVERUSE

Behavioral patterns associated with internet overuse have become a significant concern in today's society. Studies have shown that individuals who exhibit excessive internet use often display addictive behaviors similar to those observed in substance abuse disorders. These individuals may engage in compulsive internet use, neglecting responsibilities and social interactions in favor of online activities. Furthermore, they may experience withdrawal symptoms when unable to access the internet, leading to increased irritability and anxiety. Cognitive impairments, such as poor decision-making and impaired impulse control, have also been linked to internet overuse. Understanding these behavioral patterns is crucial in addressing the growing problem of internet addiction and its impact on mental health and social wellbeing. By identifying key behaviors associated with internet overuse, researchers can develop effective intervention strategies to help individuals regain control over their online habits and improve their overall quality of life.

SOCIOECONOMIC FACTORS INFLUENCING ADDICTION

Socioeconomic factors play a crucial role in influencing addiction behaviors within society. Lower socioeconomic status is often associated with increased stress, limited access to resources, and higher rates of substance abuse. Individuals facing financial hardship may turn to drugs or alcohol as a coping mechanism, seeking temporary relief from their everyday struggles. Moreover, the lack of affordable healthcare and mental health services in disadvantaged communities can hinder individuals from seeking proper treatment for their addiction issues. Additionally, the prevalence of substance abuse within low-income neighborhoods can normalize addictive behaviors, making it easier for individuals to fall into the trap of addiction. It is evident that socioeconomic disparities have a profound impact on the development, perpetuation, and treatment of addiction, highlighting the need for comprehensive interventions that address both the individual and systemic factors at play.

GENDER DIFFERENCES IN INTERNET USAGE PATTERNS

Gender differences in internet usage patterns have been a topic of interest for researchers studying the impact of technology on society. Studies have shown that men tend to use the internet more for work-related activities, such as research and communication, while women often utilize it for social networking and entertainment purposes. This divide in internet usage reflects broader societal norms and expectations regarding gender roles and interests. Understanding these patterns is crucial for addressing the potential impacts of technology on gender equality and social dynamics. By recognizing and examining these differences in internet usage, researchers can develop more targeted interventions and policies to ensure that technology benefits all members of society equally. Additionally, exploring how gender influences internet behavior can provide valuable insights into the ways in which technology can both empower and potentially exacerbate existing gender disparities.

V. THE ROLE OF SOCIAL MEDIA IN INTERNET ADDICTION

The pervasive use of social media platforms has been identified as a contributing factor to the development of internet addiction among individuals. Social media provides a constant stream of information, updates, and notifications that can easily lead to compulsive usage and a sense of FOMO (fear of missing out). The interactive nature of social media, along with features such as likes, shares, and comments, triggers dopamine release in the brain, reinforcing addictive behaviors. Studies have shown a strong association between excessive social media use and symptoms of internet addiction, including withdrawal, tolerance, and preoccupation. Moreover, the pressure to present an idealized version of oneself online can lead to feelings of inadequacy and anxiety, further fueling the need for validation through social media interactions. As such, understanding the role of social media in internet addiction is crucial in addressing the negative implications of technology on mental health in today's society.

IMPACT OF SOCIAL NETWORKING SITES

The impact of social networking sites on today's society is profound and multifaceted. On one hand, these platforms provide individuals with the opportunity to connect and communicate with others across vast distances, fostering relationships and creating communities. Social networking sites also serve as valuable tools for business networking, marketing, and professional development. However, on the flip side, the excessive use of these platforms has been linked to various negative outcomes, such as decreased mental well-being, reduced face-to-face interactions, and even addiction. The constant exposure to curated images and idealized versions of life on social media can lead to feelings of inadequacy and lower self-esteem among users. Therefore, it is essential to understand the double-edged nature of social networking sites and the implications they have on individuals' mental health and social dynamics in today's digital age.

SOCIAL MEDIA AS A PLATFORM FOR COMPARISON AND VALIDATION

Social media has become a pervasive platform for comparison and validation in today's society. Users often find themselves constantly comparing their lives, appearance, and accomplishments to those of others showcased on social media. This constant stream of comparison can lead to feelings of inadequacy, low self-esteem, and a distorted sense of reality. At the same time, social media offers the opportunity for validation through likes, comments, and shares, which can serve as a source of validation and affirmation for individuals seeking approval from their peers. However, this validation is often fleeting and can create a cycle of seeking external validation to feel worthy. It is important for individuals to be mindful of the impact that social media can have on their mental well-being and to prioritize self-validation and self-acceptance over seeking validation from external sources.

THE FEEDBACK LOOP OF SOCIAL MEDIA ENGAGEMENT

The feedback loop of social media engagement plays a crucial role in the phenomenon of internet addiction and its impact on today's society. Beginning with an individual's initial interaction with social media, the feedback loop is initiated when they receive likes, comments, and shares on their posts. This positive reinforcement leads to increased engagement with the platform as the individual seeks more validation and gratification. As this cycle continues, it can escalate to a point where the individual becomes dependent on social media for their self-worth and esteem. In the context of internet addiction, this feedback loop perpetuates a cycle of compulsive behavior and can have detrimental effects on mental health and social relationships. Therefore, understanding the feedback loop of social media engagement is crucial in addressing the broader issue of technology addiction in society.

VI. ONLINE GAMING AND INTERNET ADDICTION

The rise of online gaming has led to growing concerns about internet addiction and its impact on individuals in today's society. With the increasing accessibility and immersive nature of online games, many people are finding themselves spending excessive amounts of time engrossed in virtual worlds, leading to negative consequences in their personal and professional lives. Research has shown that internet addiction, including gaming addiction, can have detrimental effects on mental health, physical well-being, and social relationships. Moreover, individuals struggling with internet addiction may experience difficulties in controlling their impulses, prioritizing online activities over real-life responsibilities, and exhibiting withdrawal symptoms when unable to access the internet. As such, it is crucial for healthcare professionals, policymakers, and the general public to recognize the seriousness of internet addiction and work towards implementing strategies for prevention and intervention to address this growing issue.

POPULARITY OF MASSIVELY MULTIPLAYER ONLINE GAMES

The popularity of Massively Multiplayer Online Games (MMOs) has seen exponential growth in recent years, with millions of players around the world engaging in virtual adventures and competitions. This rise can be attributed to several factors, including the increasing accessibility of high-speed internet connections, the development of sophisticated gaming platforms, and the social aspect of playing with friends or meeting new individuals online. MMOs offer a unique experience that allows players to immerse themselves in captivating virtual worlds, complete with complex storylines, challenging quests, and the opportunity to interact with other players in real-time. The addictive nature of these games is fueled by the constant desire to level up, acquire rare items, and achieve virtual status within the gaming community. Researchers have raised concerns about the potential negative impact of excessive MMO play on individuals' mental health, highlighting the need for further investigation and awareness in addressing internet addiction in today's society.

PSYCHOLOGICAL REWARDS IN GAMING

Research has shown that gaming can provide various psychological rewards to players. These rewards include a sense of accomplishment, satisfaction, and mastery when completing challenging tasks within the game. This can boost self-esteem and confidence, which may translate into improved performance in real-life situations. Furthermore, gaming can also offer an escape from everyday stressors and provide a form of relaxation and entertainment. For some individuals, gaming serves as a means of social connection, allowing them to interact with others in online communities and build relationships. However, it is essential to acknowledge that excessive gaming can lead to addiction and negative consequences on mental health. By understanding the psychological rewards of gaming and its potential impacts, researchers can develop strategies to promote a healthy balance in engaging with gaming activities.

CASE STUDIES OF GAMING ADDICTION

One area of concern in the study of internet addiction is the phenomenon of gaming addiction, which has been increasingly recognized as a significant issue in today's society. Case studies of individuals struggling with gaming addiction have revealed the detrimental effects it can have on their mental, physical, and social well-being. These case studies provide valuable insights into the underlying factors contributing to gaming addiction, such as loneliness, depression, and low self-esteem. By examining these cases in depth, researchers can better understand the complexities of gaming addiction and develop targeted interventions to address this growing problem. Furthermore, analyzing these case studies can also help identify common patterns and risk factors associated with gaming addiction, allowing for the development of more effective prevention and treatment strategies. The exploration of case studies of gaming addiction is essential in gaining a comprehensive understanding of the impact of technology on individuals' lives and society as a whole.

VII. CYBER-RELATIONSHIPS AND EMOTIONAL DEPENDENCY

Cyber-relationships have become increasingly prevalent in today's society, offering individuals the opportunity to connect with others on a virtual platform. However, this digital connectivity has also led to concerns regarding emotional dependency. Research suggests that individuals who engage in online relationships may develop a sense of emotional reliance on their digital connections, potentially leading to a lack of emotional fulfillment in face-to-face interactions. This can be particularly problematic when individuals prioritize their online relationships over real-life connections, resulting in social withdrawal and isolation. Moreover, the instantaneous nature of communication in cyber-relationships may facilitate the development of intense emotional bonds that could exacerbate feelings of dependency. As technology continues to advance, it is crucial to recognize the potential impact of cyber-relationships on emotional well-being and to establish boundaries to maintain a healthy balance between virtual and real-world connections.

FORMATION OF ONLINE RELATIONSHIPS

Formation of online relationships has become increasingly common in today's digital society, with individuals connecting and establishing social bonds through various online platforms. These relationships can range from casual friendships to more intimate connections, often transcending geographical boundaries and time zones. The allure of forming relationships online lies in the convenience and accessibility it offers, allowing individuals to interact with others from the comfort of their own homes. However, the ease of forming online relationships can also lead to challenges, such as the difficulty in discerning the authenticity and sincerity of interactions. This duality of online relationships underscores the need for individuals to exercise caution and discernment when establishing connections in the digital realm, as well as the importance of nurturing and maintaining genuine relationships both online and offline. Understanding the dynamics of online relationships is crucial in navigating the complexities of modern social interactions in a technology-driven world.

EMOTIONAL INVESTMENT IN VIRTUAL INTERACTIONS

In today's digital age, the phenomenon of emotional investment in virtual interactions has become increasingly prevalent and consequential. Individuals now form deep connections with others online through social media platforms, online gaming communities, and virtual reality environments. This emotional investment is fueled by the human need for connection and belonging, leading to the blurring of boundaries between the physical and digital worlds. However, this increasing reliance on virtual interactions comes with its own set of challenges and implications. Research suggests that excessive emotional investment in virtual interactions can lead to internet addiction, social isolation, and a decline in real-world relationships. As such, it is imperative for society to recognize the double-sided nature of technology and its impact on individual well-being. Striking a balance between virtual and physical interactions is essential in navigating the complexities of modern-day connectivity.

CONSEQUENCES OF CYBER-RELATIONSHIPS ON REAL-LIFE SOCIAL SKILLS

The consequences of cyber-relationships on real-life social skills are a complex and multi-faceted issue that requires careful examination. While some argue that online interactions can enhance social skills by providing individuals with the opportunity to practice communication in a low-pressure environment, others suggest that excessive reliance on digital communication can lead to a deterioration in face-to-face social skills. Research indicates that individuals who spend a significant amount of time engaging in cyber-relationships may struggle with nonverbal cues, emotional intelligence, and conflict resolution in real-life interactions. This can have far-reaching implications for personal relationships, professional success, and overall well-being. As technology continues to shape the way we communicate and interact with others, it is crucial to understand the impact of cyber-relationships on real-life social skills and develop strategies to promote healthy and balanced social interactions in the digital age.

VIII. THE INTERNET AS AN INFORMATION SOURCE

In the modern era, the internet has emerged as a primary source of information for individuals across the globe. Its unparalleled accessibility and vast array of resources make it a valuable tool for research and communication. However, the reliance on the internet as an information source raises concerns about the quality and reliability of the information being consumed. The sheer volume of data available online can be overwhelming, leading to difficulties in discerning accurate information from misinformation. This challenge is exacerbated by the rise of fake news and biased sources that can easily be disseminated through online platforms. As such, it is imperative for individuals to develop critical thinking skills and employ discernment when navigating the internet for information. By doing so, users can effectively sift through the vast sea of data to access reliable and trustworthy sources, thus maximizing the benefits of the internet as an information source while minimizing the risks associated with misinformation.

THE OVERLOAD OF INFORMATION AVAILABILITY

In today's digital age, the overwhelming amount of information available at our fingertips poses a significant challenge in terms of information overload. With the vast array of online resources, social media platforms, and news outlets constantly bombarding individuals with information, it is easy to become inundated and overwhelmed. This overload of information availability can lead to issues such as cognitive overload, decreased productivity, and difficulty in decision-making. The sheer volume of data can make it challenging for individuals to discern what information is relevant and accurate, leading to a sense of confusion and disorientation. As technology continues to advance and information becomes increasingly accessible, it is crucial for individuals to develop effective strategies for filtering and evaluating the information they encounter to prevent the negative impacts of information overload on their cognitive well-being and overall functioning in today's society.

CHALLENGES IN DISCERNING RELIABLE INFORMATION

In the realm of internet addiction and its impact on today's society, one of the primary challenges researchers face is discerning reliable information amidst the vast sea of digital content. With the proliferation of fake news, misinformation, and biased sources online, distinguishing credible sources from unreliable ones has become a daunting task. The availability of information at our fingertips has led to an overwhelming amount of data, making it difficult to separate fact from fiction. Additionally, the rapid dissemination of information on the internet can lead to the amplification of falsehoods, creating a culture of misinformation that is hard to combat. As researchers strive to uncover the true effects of internet addiction on individuals and society, navigating through the web of unreliable information poses a significant obstacle that must be addressed with caution and critical analysis.

THE PARADOX OF CHOICE IN THE DIGITAL AGE

The paradox of choice in the digital age stems from the abundance of options available to individuals in virtually every aspect of their lives. While having numerous choices can be empowering, it can also lead to decision paralysis, anxiety, and dissatisfaction. In the realm of technology, the internet offers an overwhelming array of products, services, and information, making it challenging for individuals to make informed decisions. This phenomenon is exacerbated by the personalization algorithms used by tech companies, which further tailor choices to individual preferences, creating a filter bubble that limits exposure to alternative viewpoints. As a result, individuals may find themselves trapped in a cycle of excessive consumption and comparison, leading to a sense of inadequacy and frustration. Understanding and addressing the paradox of choice is crucial in mitigating the negative impact of internet addiction on individuals and society as a whole.

IX. THE INTERNET AND WORK PRODUCTIVITY

The impact of the internet on work productivity is a topic of growing concern in today's society. While the internet has revolutionized the way we work, providing access to a wealth of information and resources at our fingertips, it has also introduced new challenges that can hinder productivity. One of the main issues is the temptation of constant connectivity, with employees often struggling to disconnect from work outside of office hours. This can lead to burnout and decreased productivity in the long run. Additionally, the easy access to distractions on the internet, such as social media and entertainment sites, can further detract from work focus and efficiency. Therefore, it is crucial for organizations to establish boundaries and promote a healthy work-life balance to ensure that the benefits of the internet do not outweigh its negative impact on work productivity.

INTERNET AS A TOOL FOR EFFICIENCY

The internet has become an invaluable tool for increasing efficiency in various aspects of modern society. In today's digital
age, the internet facilitates seamless communication, collaboration, and information sharing, enabling organizations to
streamline their operations and enhance productivity. By leveraging online platforms, businesses can automate repetitive
tasks, access real-time data, and connect with global markets,
leading to cost savings and improved performance. Moreover,
the internet enables individuals to access a wealth of resources,
such as online courses, research articles, and professional networks, that can enhance their skills and knowledge. However,
while the internet offers numerous benefits in terms of efficiency,
it is crucial to recognize the potential downsides, such as information overload, distraction, and cybersecurity risks, that can
result from excessive reliance on digital tools. Therefore, it is
essential for individuals and organizations to strike a balance
between utilizing the internet for efficiency and managing its
potential negative impacts.

DISTRACTIONS AND MULTITASKING ONLINE

Distractions and multitasking online pose significant challenges in today's society, especially in the realm of academia and research. The constant bombardment of notifications, emails, and social media updates can derail focus and hinder productivity. Studies have shown that multitasking can actually decrease efficiency and lead to a decrease in the quality of work produced. In the context of research, the ability to concentrate on a single task and delve deep into a topic is crucial for generating new insights and contributing to knowledge. Therefore, it is essential for researchers to develop strategies to minimize distractions and prioritize tasks effectively. Techniques such as time-blocking, setting specific periods for focused work, and utilizing productivity tools can help individuals manage distractions and enhance their research output. By acknowledging the detrimental effects of multitasking online, researchers can strive to cultivate a more focused and productive work environment.

IMPACT ON WORK-LIFE BALANCE

The impact of internet addiction on work-life balance is a critical issue facing today's society. Excessive use of technology can lead to blurred boundaries between work and personal life, causing individuals to struggle with maintaining a healthy balance. This imbalance can result in increased stress, burnout, and decreased productivity in the workplace as individuals find it challenging to disconnect from their digital devices. Furthermore, the constant connectivity afforded by technology can lead to feelings of overwhelming pressure to always be available, making it difficult for individuals to fully engage in leisure activities or spend quality time with loved ones. As a result, addressing the negative effects of internet addiction on work-life balance is crucial for promoting overall well-being and productivity in today's fast-paced and digitally-driven world.

X. EDUCATIONAL IMPLICATIONS OF INTERNET ADDICTION

The educational implications of internet addiction are a growing concern in today's society. As more and more individuals, including students, become dependent on the internet for information and communication, the negative effects of this addiction on academic performance are becoming evident. Research has shown that students who are addicted to the internet often struggle with time management, leading to procrastination and a decline in productivity. This can result in poor grades, decreased motivation, and a lack of focus in the classroom. Moreover, internet addiction can also have detrimental effects on students' social skills and overall well-being, further impacting their ability to succeed academically. Therefore, it is crucial for educators to be aware of the signs of internet addiction and to implement strategies to address this issue in order to support students in achieving their academic potential and overall success.

ONLINE LEARNING AND STUDENT ENGAGEMENT

Student engagement in online learning has been a topic of great interest and concern in recent years, as the shift towards digital platforms for education continues to grow. While online learning offers convenience and flexibility for students, it can also present challenges in terms of maintaining high levels of engagement. Effective strategies must be implemented to keep students actively involved in their online courses, such as incorporating interactive elements, fostering a sense of community through discussion forums, and providing timely feedback on assignments. Research has shown that engaged students are more likely to succeed academically and feel a stronger sense of connection to their learning experience. Therefore, it is crucial for educators to prioritize student engagement in online learning environments to ensure that learners are fully invested in their educational journey and able to reach their full potential.

DISTRACTION AND ACADEMIC PERFORMANCE

Distraction has become a prevalent issue in today's society, particularly among students, affecting their academic performance. The constant access to technology, such as smartphones and social media, has led to an increase in distractions that students face while studying or in the classroom. These distractions not only impact their ability to focus and retain information but also hinder their overall academic achievements. Research has shown that students who are easily distracted by technology tend to have lower grades and struggle to meet academic expectations. Therefore, addressing the issue of distraction and finding effective strategies to minimize its impact on students' academic performance is crucial. By understanding the negative effects of distractions on academic success, educators and policymakers can work towards creating a more conducive learning environment that fosters concentration and enhances learning outcomes.

THE DIGITAL DIVIDE IN EDUCATION

The digital divide in education remains a pressing issue in today's society, with disparities in access to technology and digital literacy skills widening the gap between privileged and marginalized populations. As technology continues to play a vital role in education, those who lack adequate resources or training are at a significant disadvantage. This not only affects academic performance but also hinders opportunities for future success in the digital age. Bridging this divide requires targeted interventions at both the individual and systemic levels, including providing equitable access to devices and internet connectivity, as well as implementing comprehensive digital literacy programs. By addressing these issues, we can work towards creating a more inclusive and egalitarian educational environment that empowers all students to thrive in a technology-driven world. It is imperative that policymakers, educators, and stakeholders collaborate to ensure that no one is left behind in the digital era.

XI. THE ECONOMIC IMPACT OF INTERNET ADDICTION

The economic impact of internet addiction is a significant concern in today's society. Individuals who struggle with internet addiction often experience a decline in productivity, leading to decreased work performance and potential job loss. Employers may also incur costs related to absenteeism, decreased focus, and increased healthcare expenses for employees struggling with this addiction. In addition, the excessive use of online shopping, gaming, or social media can lead to financial strain, as individuals may spend exorbitant amounts of money on these activities, leading to debt and financial insecurity. The economic consequences of internet addiction can extend beyond the individual level to impact businesses, healthcare systems, and overall economic growth. Therefore, it is imperative for policymakers, employers, and healthcare professionals to address the economic ramifications of internet addiction and implement strategies to mitigate its impact on the economy.

COST TO EMPLOYERS FROM REDUCED PRODUCTIVITY

Employers face significant costs from reduced productivity due to internet addiction in today's society. Employees who spend excessive amounts of time on the internet engaging in non-work-related activities may experience decreased efficiency, poor time management, and lack of focus on job tasks. This can lead to missed deadlines, errors in work, and overall lower quality output. As a result, employers may need to invest in additional resources to compensate for the lost productivity, such as hiring temporary workers or providing extra training for struggling employees. Moreover, the negative impact of internet addiction on employee morale and teamwork can further hinder productivity in the workplace. Ultimately, the cost to employers from reduced productivity caused by internet addiction highlights the need for effective strategies to address and prevent this issue in the modern workforce.

THE MARKET OF ATTENTION ECONOMY

The market of attention economy has become increasingly significant in today's digital age, where individuals are bombarded with endless streams of information vying for their attention. With the rise of social media, online advertising, and content consumption, attention has become a valuable commodity that companies and individuals alike are competing for. This market of attention economy has led to the proliferation of clickbait, sensationalist content, and addictive online behaviors aimed at capturing and maintaining the attention of users. As a result, internet addiction has become a growing concern, with individuals spending excessive amounts of time online, often to the detriment of their physical and mental well-being. Understanding the dynamics of the attention economy and its impact on society is crucial in addressing the pervasive issue of internet addiction and promoting healthy digital habits among individuals.

FINANCIAL IMPLICATIONS FOR INDIVIDUALS

Financial implications for individuals affected by internet addiction can be significant and multifaceted. From a psychological standpoint, the compulsive need to be online can lead to decreased productivity, resulting in potential job loss or decreased academic performance. This can have a direct impact on an individual's income and financial stability. Additionally, excessive online shopping or gambling behaviors can lead to substantial financial burdens, as individuals may accrue debt or spend beyond their means. The cost of seeking treatment for internet addiction, such as therapy or counseling, can also add up over time. Furthermore, the constant need for the latest technology or gadgets to feed the addiction can strain one's finances. In conclusion, internet addiction can have detrimental effects on an individual's financial well-being, highlighting the need for greater awareness and support in managing this issue.

XII. HEALTH CONSEQUENCES OF EXCESSIVE INTERNET USE

Excessive internet use has been linked to a range of health consequences that can impact individuals in various ways. Physical health problems such as poor posture, eye strain, and headaches are common among those who spend long hours in front of screens. Additionally, excessive internet use has been linked to sleep disturbances, with disrupted sleep patterns affecting overall well-being and cognitive function. Furthermore, the psychological effects of internet addiction can be profound, contributing to increased levels of stress, anxiety, and depression. These mental health issues can not only diminish one's quality of life but also lead to social withdrawal and decreased productivity. It is crucial for researchers and healthcare professionals to recognize the negative health implications associated with excessive internet use and to develop effective strategies for prevention and intervention to promote healthier online behaviors and overall well-being in today's society.

PHYSICAL HEALTH RISKS

Physical health risks associated with internet addiction are a growing concern in today's society. Excessive screen time and sedentary behavior linked to internet addiction can lead to a range of health problems, including obesity, musculoskeletal issues, and sleep disturbances. Research has shown that prolonged sitting while using electronic devices can increase the risk of developing chronic conditions such as heart disease, diabetes, and hypertension. Furthermore, the blue light emitted from screens can disrupt the circadian rhythm, affecting sleep quality and overall well-being. These physical health risks not only impact individuals struggling with internet addiction but also have broader societal implications. Addressing these concerns requires a multifaceted approach that includes promoting physical activity, implementing screen time limits, and raising awareness about the potential consequences of excessive internet use on health. By recognizing and addressing these risks, we can work towards creating a healthier and more balanced relationship with technology.

MENTAL HEALTH CONCERNS

Mental health concerns stemming from internet addiction are a significant issue in today's society. The constant use of technology can lead to anxiety, depression, and other mental health disorders. This addiction can cause individuals to isolate themselves, neglect their responsibilities, and experience mood swings. It also affects their relationships and overall well-being. Furthermore, the pressure to constantly be connected online can elevate stress levels and lead to burnout. Research shows that excessive use of the internet can change brain structures and neural pathways, contributing to mental health issues. To address this issue, it is essential to promote digital detoxes, mindfulness practices, and healthy tech habits. By acknowledging the impact of technology on mental health and implementing strategies to mitigate the negative effects, individuals can regain control over their well-being and overall quality of life.

SLEEP DISTURBANCES AND INTERNET ADDICTION

Recent research has shown a concerning link between sleep disturbances and internet addiction, highlighting the negative impact of excessive screen time on individuals' overall well-being. The proliferation of digital devices has led to a cultural shift, with many individuals spending extended hours online, often at the expense of adequate sleep. Poor sleep quality and disrupted sleep patterns can contribute to the development and exacerbation of internet addiction, creating a vicious cycle that is detrimental to one's mental and physical health. Understanding the complex interplay between sleep disturbances and internet addiction is crucial for developing effective prevention and intervention strategies. By addressing underlying sleep issues and promoting healthy technology use habits, individuals can better manage their online behaviors and mitigate the risk of internet addiction. Through interdisciplinary research and collaboration, we can work towards fostering a balanced relationship with technology in today's society.

XIII. INTERNET ADDICTION AND PERSONAL RELATIONSHIPS

Internet addiction can have a profound impact on personal relationships in today's society. Individuals who struggle with internet addiction may prioritize online interactions over face-to-face communication, leading to strained relationships with friends, family members, and romantic partners. This phenomenon can result in feelings of isolation, mistrust, and neglect among those affected by excessive internet use. Moreover, the constant need for online validation and engagement can detract from the quality of in-person interactions, hindering the development of strong emotional connections. As a result, relationships may suffer from a lack of intimacy, communication, and genuine connection. It is essential for individuals with internet addiction to recognize the negative consequences it can have on their personal relationships and seek help in order to cultivate healthier and more fulfilling interactions with those around them.

IMPACT ON FAMILY DYNAMICS

The impact of internet addiction on family dynamics is a critical issue that warrants attention in today's society. As individuals become consumed by their online activities, the traditional roles and responsibilities within families may become disrupted. Parents may struggle to establish boundaries with their children, as devices and screens become constant companions. Sibling relationships may be strained as attention and time are diverted to virtual interactions rather than real-life connections. Moreover, the rise of cyberbullying and online predators poses a significant threat to the safety and well-being of family members. These challenges can lead to increased conflict, decreased communication, and a breakdown in trust within the family unit. It is imperative for researchers and policymakers to address these issues comprehensively to protect the foundation of society - the family.

ROMANTIC RELATIONSHIPS AND ONLINE INFIDELITY

Romantic relationships in the digital age have been significantly impacted by the prevalence of online infidelity. With the ease of access to various platforms and social media, individuals are more susceptible to engaging in extramarital affairs or emotional connections outside their primary relationship. The anonymity and convenience provided by the internet create a breeding ground for infidelity to thrive, with individuals seeking emotional fulfillment and excitement outside their committed partnerships. This shift in the dynamics of romantic relationships raises concerns about trust, communication, and boundaries in modern society. Couples must navigate these challenges by fostering open dialogues, establishing clear expectations, and acknowledging the risks associated with online interactions. Addressing the issue of online infidelity requires a holistic approach that incorporates individual accountability, technological boundaries, and relationship reinforcement to safeguard the integrity and longevity of romantic partnerships in today's digital landscape.

SOCIAL ISOLATION AND LONELINESS

Social isolation and loneliness are increasingly prevalent issues in today's society, exacerbated by the rise of technology and social media. While these platforms are designed to connect people, they can also paradoxically contribute to feelings of isolation. Research has shown that excessive use of technology often leads to decreased face-to-face interactions and weakened social ties, ultimately increasing feelings of loneliness. The constant exposure to curated versions of others' lives on social media can also result in a sense of inadequacy and disconnection. Moreover, the anonymity and superficial nature of online interactions may inhibit the development of deep, meaningful relationships. It is crucial for individuals to strike a balance between their online and offline interactions to combat social isolation and cultivate authentic connections. Addressing these issues is essential for promoting mental well-being and fostering a sense of belonging in our increasingly digital world.

XIV. LEGAL AND ETHICAL CONSIDERATIONS

As the prevalence of internet addiction continues to rise, it has become crucial to examine the legal and ethical implications surrounding this issue. From a legal standpoint, there is a growing need for regulations and policies to address the harmful effects of excessive internet use on individuals and society. Laws regarding data privacy, online harassment, and child protection must be enforced to mitigate the risks associated with internet addiction. Furthermore, ethical considerations come into play when discussing the responsibility of internet service providers and tech companies in promoting healthy online behavior. It is essential to consider the ethical implications of online advertising, data collection, and the design of addictive technologies. By addressing these legal and ethical concerns, policymakers can work towards creating a safer and more responsible digital environment for all users. As researchers and practitioners in the field of psychology, it is our duty to advocate for these considerations and contribute to the development of effective strategies for preventing and addressing internet addiction.

INTERNET PRIVACY CONCERNS

Internet privacy concerns have become a prominent issue in to-day's society as technology continues to advance. With the widespread use of social media, online shopping, and various digital platforms, individuals are increasingly sharing personal information that can easily be exploited by malicious entities. The collection of data by companies for targeted advertising and the potential for data breaches have raised alarms regarding the security and privacy of online users. This has led to a grow-ing awareness of the importance of protecting one's online pri-vacy, with calls for stricter regulations and enhanced security measures. As individuals navigate the digital landscape, it is crucial for them to be cautious about the information they share online and to be aware of the potential risks associated with the misuse of their personal data. Emphasizing the need for a bal-ance between convenience and privacy, it is imperative for so-ciety to address these concerns to safeguard individual rights in the digital age.

CYBERBULLYING AND LEGAL RAMIFICATIONS

Cyberbullying has increasingly become a pressing issue in to-day's society, with individuals using the anonymity of the internet to harass, threaten, or intimidate others. The legal ramifications of cyberbullying are complex, as they often involve navigating through various laws and regulations that may not have caught up with the fast-paced nature of online interactions. While some countries have enacted specific legislations to address cyberbullying, many still lack comprehensive measures to adequately protect individuals from online abuse. Furthermore, the anonymous nature of the internet poses challenges in identifying and holding perpetrators accountable. In cases where cyberbullying escalates to serious consequences such as mental health issues or even suicide, questions of liability and culpability arise. As society grapples with the impact of cyberbullying, legal frameworks need to evolve to provide better protection for victims and hold perpetrators accountable for their actions.

ETHICAL IMPLICATIONS OF DIGITAL FOOTPRINTS

The ethical implications of digital footprints are a complex and multifaceted issue that requires careful consideration in today's digital age. As individuals engage in online activities, they leave behind a trail of data that can be collected, analyzed, and potentially used for various purposes, both beneficial and harmful. On one hand, digital footprints can enhance personalized services, improve marketing strategies, and advance research in various fields. However, on the other hand, they raise concerns about privacy, surveillance, data security, and potential discrimination based on the information collected. It is imperative for individuals, organizations, and policymakers to navigate this ethical minefield responsibly, ensuring that digital footprints are used in a manner that respects privacy, protects data security, and promotes transparency. By addressing these ethical considerations, we can better harness the power of digital footprints while minimizing the risks associated with their use.

XV. INTERNET ADDICTION AND PUBLIC POLICY

Internet addiction is a growing concern in today's society, with individuals of all ages spending excessive amounts of time online, leading to negative consequences on their physical and mental well-being. Public policy plays a crucial role in addressing this issue by implementing regulations and guidelines to protect individuals from the harmful effects of internet addiction. Policies can focus on promoting digital literacy and awareness, providing resources for those struggling with addiction, and regulating the content and advertising on online platforms. By addressing internet addiction through public policy, governments can work towards creating a healthier and more balanced relationship with technology in society. It is essential for policymakers to collaborate with experts in the field to develop evidence-based strategies that effectively address the complex nature of internet addiction and its impact on individuals and communities.

GOVERNMENTAL RESPONSES TO INTERNET ADDICTION

Governmental responses to the growing issue of internet addiction have been varied and evolving over the years. At the beginning, many governments were slow to recognize internet addiction as a legitimate concern, often dismissing it as a personal responsibility issue. However, as the negative consequences of excessive internet use became more apparent, governments around the world began to take action. Some countries have implemented laws or regulations to limit internet access, especially for minors, while others have focused on educational programs and awareness campaigns. Still, there are critics who argue that governmental intervention may infringe on individuals' rights or be ineffective in addressing the root causes of addiction. Despite these challenges, it is clear that government involvement is crucial in combating internet addiction and protecting the well-being of society as a whole.

REGULATION OF ONLINE CONTENT

The regulation of online content has become a critical issue in today's digital age. With the proliferation of social media platforms and the easy dissemination of information, there is a growing concern about the quality and accuracy of online content. In order to maintain the integrity of information available on the internet, regulations must be put in place to ensure that content is reliable and trustworthy. However, the challenge lies in finding a balance between protecting freedom of speech and preventing the spread of misinformation. Striking this balance requires careful consideration of legal and ethical principles, as well as the responsibilities of online platforms in controlling the content shared on their sites. As technology continues to evolve, it is essential for policymakers to adapt regulations to address the ever-changing landscape of online content and its impact on society.

PUBLIC HEALTH CAMPAIGNS AND EDUCATION

Public health campaigns and education play a crucial role in addressing the issue of internet addiction in today's society. By raising awareness about the negative impacts of excessive internet use on physical and mental health, these campaigns can help individuals recognize the signs of addiction and seek appropriate help. Educational programs can also provide strategies for managing screen time and developing healthier online habits. Furthermore, public health campaigns can work to destigmatize seeking help for internet addiction, encouraging individuals to reach out for support without fear of judgment. By combining education with targeted messaging, these campaigns have the potential to make a significant impact in reducing the prevalence of internet addiction and improving the overall well-being of individuals in society. Through a coordinated effort, public health campaigns can help to address the double-sided nature of technology and promote a more balanced use of digital resources.

XVI. TREATMENT AND INTERVENTION STRATEGIES

In addressing the issue of internet addiction and its widespread impact on society, it is essential to explore effective treatment and intervention strategies. One approach involves cognitive-behavioral therapy (CBT), which focuses on identifying and changing maladaptive thoughts and behaviors related to internet use. This therapeutic technique aims to help individuals develop coping skills and self-regulation strategies to manage their online activities. Additionally, family therapy can play a crucial role in the treatment process by addressing underlying family dynamics that may contribute to addictive behaviors. Furthermore, incorporating mindfulness-based interventions can help individuals cultivate awareness and self-control over their internet usage. By integrating a variety of treatment modalities, tailored to the individual's needs, clinicians can effectively address internet addiction and promote healthier technology use in today's society.

COUNSELING AND THERAPY OPTIONS

Traditional therapies such as CBT have been effective in treating addiction by identifying negative thought patterns and replacing them with healthier coping mechanisms. Additionally, family therapy can be beneficial in addressing underlying family dynamics that may contribute to addictive behaviors. However, as technology continues to evolve, online counseling and virtual therapy sessions have emerged as convenient alternatives for individuals struggling with internet addiction. These online platforms offer flexibility and accessibility, making therapy more convenient for those who may have trouble attending in-person sessions. By utilizing a combination of traditional counseling methods and innovative online options, individuals can receive comprehensive support in overcoming internet addiction and improving their overall well-being.

SUPPORT GROUPS AND COMMUNITY RESOURCES

In addressing Internet addiction's impact on society, support groups and community resources play a crucial role in providing assistance to individuals struggling with this issue. Support groups offer a platform for individuals to share experiences, provide emotional support, and offer practical advice on managing internet usage. These groups create a sense of community and understanding among members, reducing feelings of isolation and stigma. Additionally, community resources such as counseling services and educational programs can equip individuals with the necessary tools to address their addictive behaviors effectively. By working in tandem, support groups and community resources can empower individuals to make positive changes in their lives and break free from the grasp of internet addiction. As researchers and practitioners continue to explore effective interventions, the collaboration between support groups and community resources remains essential in addressing this growing societal concern.

PREVENTATIVE MEASURES AND EDUCATION

To combat the growing issue of internet addiction in today's society, preventative measures and education are crucial. One effective strategy is implementing awareness programs in schools and workplaces to educate individuals about the signs and consequences of excessive internet use. This can help individuals recognize problematic behaviors early on and seek help before addiction develops. Additionally, promoting healthy screen time habits and digital detox practices can help individuals maintain a balanced relationship with technology. Providing resources for mental health support and addiction counseling can also be beneficial in addressing internet addiction. By emphasizing prevention and education, society can work towards reducing the prevalence of internet addiction and mitigating its negative impact on individuals and communities. These measures are essential in promoting a healthier relationship with technology and ensuring the well-being of future generations.

XVII. THE ROLE OF TECHNOLOGY COMPANIES

Technology companies play a crucial role in the prevalence of internet addiction and its impact on today's society. These companies design and develop platforms and devices that are specifically engineered to capture users' attention for extended periods. The business models of many technology companies are based on maximizing user engagement and increasing time spent on their platforms, which can lead to addictive behaviors among users. Furthermore, these companies often employ tactics such as personalized notifications, recommendations, and rewards to keep users hooked. While technology companies argue that their products enhance connectivity and productivity, the negative consequences of excessive technology use cannot be overlooked. As technology continues to advance, it is imperative for these companies to take responsibility for the societal impacts of their products and to prioritize the well-being of their users over profit margins.

CORPORATE RESPONSIBILITY AND ETHICAL DESIGN

Corporate responsibility and ethical design play a crucial role in the development and implementation of technologies, especially in the context of internet addiction. Companies must consider the ethical implications of their designs, ensuring that they prioritize the well-being of users over profits. By incorporating ethical design practices, companies can mitigate the risks of internet addiction and promote healthy usage of technology. Corporate responsibility goes beyond mere compliance with regulations; it involves a commitment to upholding ethical standards and ensuring that the products and services offered are beneficial to society as a whole. By embracing corporate responsibility and ethical design principles, companies can contribute to a more sustainable and socially responsible technological landscape, ultimately helping to address the challenges posed by internet addiction in today's society.

IMPLEMENTING USAGE LIMITS AND PARENTAL CONTROLS

The implementation of usage limits and parental controls is a crucial aspect in addressing the issue of internet addiction within today's society. By setting boundaries on the amount of time individuals can spend online and restricting access to certain websites or content, parents can help regulate and monitor their children's online activities. This proactive approach also extends to adults who may struggle with excessive internet use, providing them with tools to self-regulate and maintain a healthy balance between virtual and real-world interactions. Additionally, the enforcement of usage limits and parental controls can prevent individuals from falling into the trap of endless scrolling and compulsive online behavior. By promoting responsible internet usage through the implementation of these measures, we can mitigate the negative consequences of internet addiction and foster a more balanced relationship with technology in our daily lives.

TRANSPARENCY IN DATA COLLECTION AND USAGE

Transparency in data collection and usage is crucial in addressing the ethical challenges surrounding internet addiction. By openly disclosing how data is collected, stored, and utilized, companies can build trust with users and demonstrate accountability. This transparency can also help individuals make informed decisions about their online behavior and the potential consequences of excessive internet use. However, the flip side of this transparency is the potential for data misuse or exploitation by third parties. Therefore, it is essential for organizations to not only be transparent about their data practices but also to implement robust security measures to protect user information. By striking a balance between transparency and data security, society can mitigate the risks associated with internet addiction and ensure that individuals can navigate the online world safely and responsibly.

XVIII. THE POSITIVE ASPECTS OF INTERNET USE

While internet addiction poses significant challenges in today's society, it is also essential to acknowledge the positive aspects of internet use. The internet provides access to a vast amount of information and resources that can aid in education, research, and professional development. It facilitates communication and collaboration among individuals, allowing for global networking and knowledge sharing. Additionally, the internet provides platforms for creativity, innovation, and entrepreneurship, enabling individuals to showcase their talents and ideas to a broader audience. Furthermore, the internet has revolutionized industries such as healthcare, finance, and entertainment, offering new opportunities for growth and advancement. By recognizing and harnessing the positive aspects of internet use, society can maximize the benefits of technology while mitigating the risks of internet addiction.

FOSTERING GLOBAL CONNECTIONS

In today's interconnected world, fostering global connections has become essential for societal development and progress. The advent of technology, particularly the internet, has revolutionized the way individuals and communities interact on a global scale. By breaking down geographical barriers and facilitating instant communication, the internet has enabled the seamless exchange of ideas, information, and resources across borders. This interconnectedness has had a profound impact on various aspects of society, from education and business to politics and culture. However, while these global connections have brought about undeniable benefits, they have also raised concerns about privacy, cybersecurity, and the spread of misinformation. It is imperative for individuals and institutions to navigate this digital landscape carefully, leveraging the power of global connections while also being mindful of the potential risks and challenges that come with it. Through thoughtful and responsible engagement with technology, we can harness the full potential of global connectivity for the betterment of society as a whole.

ACCESS TO EDUCATION AND RESOURCES

Access to education and resources plays a crucial role in shaping individuals' abilities to navigate the digital world and avoid the pitfalls of internet addiction. With the rapid advancements in technology, ensuring that everyone has equal opportunities to educate themselves about the risks of excessive internet use is paramount. Schools and educational institutions must provide comprehensive programs that address digital literacy and responsible online behavior. Additionally, access to resources such as counseling services and support groups for those struggling with internet addiction is essential in mitigating its impact on today's society. By promoting awareness and providing the necessary tools for individuals to make informed decisions about their online habits, we can work towards creating a healthier digital environment for all members of society. Ultimately, proactive measures in education and resource allocation are key in addressing the double-sided nature of technology in contemporary society.

PLATFORMS FOR CREATIVITY AND SELF-EXPRESSION

Platforms for creativity and self-expression play a crucial role in today's society, providing individuals with the means to express themselves in unique and innovative ways. Social media platforms, such as Instagram and Twitter, allow users to share their thoughts, ideas, and creativity with a global audience instantly. These platforms have also become a source of inspiration for many, fostering a sense of community and camaraderie among users. However, the downside of these platforms lies in the potential for addiction and negative impacts on mental health. Research has shown that excessive use of social media can lead to feelings of inadequacy, anxiety, and depression. Therefore, it is essential to strike a balance between utilizing online platforms for creativity and self-expression while also being mindful of the potential risks associated with overuse.

XIX. BALANCING ONLINE AND OFFLINE LIVES

In the digital age, individuals must learn to strike a delicate balance between their online and offline lives. The rapid advancement of technology has made it easier for people to stay connected virtually, but this constant connectivity can often lead to internet addiction. As more and more individuals become engrossed in their online lives, they may neglect their responsibilities in the physical world, leading to negative consequences for their well-being and relationships. Finding a balance between the digital and real world is crucial for maintaining a healthy lifestyle. By setting boundaries for online activities, managing screen time, and prioritizing face-to-face interactions, individuals can prevent internet addiction and ensure that they are fully present in their offline lives. Balancing online and offline lives is essential for promoting overall mental and emotional well-being in today's society.

STRATEGIES FOR HEALTHY INTERNET USE

Strategies for healthy internet use are crucial in today's digital age, where individuals are constantly bombarded with online distractions. One effective strategy is setting specific time limits for internet usage, allowing individuals to balance their online activities with other aspects of their lives. Implementing regular breaks from screens can also help prevent physical strain and mental fatigue. Additionally, practicing mindfulness while using the internet can increase awareness of online habits and promote intentional and focused browsing. Developing hobbies and interests offline can further reduce the reliance on the internet for entertainment and relaxation. By incorporating these strategies into daily routines, individuals can cultivate a healthier relationship with the internet, mitigating the risks of internet addiction and its detrimental impact on mental health and well-being in today's society.

IMPORTANCE OF OFFLINE HOBBIES AND ACTIVITIES

Engaging in offline hobbies and activities is crucial in today's society dominated by technology. These pursuits provide individuals with a much-needed break from the constant connectivity and screen time that characterize modern life. By participating in offline hobbies, individuals can disconnect from the digital world, allowing them to recharge, relax, and focus on activities that stimulate creativity and personal growth. Offline hobbies such as painting, hiking, gardening, or sports not only offer mental and physical health benefits but also promote social interactions and skill development. These activities enhance overall well-being and contribute to a balanced lifestyle, counteracting the negative effects of internet addiction. Therefore, it is imperative for individuals to prioritize offline hobbies and activities as a means of fostering a healthy and fulfilling existence amidst the pervasive influence of technology.

MINDFULNESS AND DIGITAL DETOX

Mindfulness and digital detox have emerged as crucial strategies in combating internet addiction and addressing its impact on individuals and society. Mindfulness practices, such as meditation and deep breathing exercises, can help individuals develop self-awareness and self-regulation, enabling them to better manage their online behaviors and resist the lure of constant digital engagement. Moreover, mindfulness fosters a sense of presence in the moment, reducing the likelihood of mindless scrolling or compulsive usage of digital devices. On the other hand, a digital detox involves intentionally disconnecting from technology for a period of time to reset one's relationship with digital devices and reevaluate priorities. By taking breaks from screens and engaging in offline activities, individuals can regain a sense of balance, reduce stress, and improve their overall well-being. Ultimately, integrating mindfulness practices and digital detox into daily routines can promote healthier relationships with technology and mitigate the negative consequences of internet addiction in today's society.

XX. THE FUTURE OF INTERNET ADDICTION

One of the pressing issues facing society today is the escalating problem of internet addiction. As technology advances at a rapid pace, the lure of constant connectivity and instant gratification has led to a rise in individuals struggling with compulsive internet use. This phenomenon not only impacts the mental health and well-being of individuals but also poses challenges to societal norms and relationships. The future of internet addiction remains uncertain, with potential consequences ranging from increased isolation and reduced productivity to potential regulatory measures to curb excessive internet usage. As researchers delve deeper into the complexities of internet addiction, it is imperative to develop strategies for prevention and intervention to mitigate the negative effects on individuals and society as a whole. By addressing the root causes and implementing targeted interventions, we can navigate the evolving landscape of technology and foster healthier relationships with the digital world.

PREDICTIONS ON TECHNOLOGICAL ADVANCEMENTS

Predictions on technological advancements indicate a future filled with possibilities and challenges. As we move towards an era of artificial intelligence, quantum computing, and IoT, the potential for innovation seems limitless. These advancements hold promise for revolutionizing industries, improving healthcare services, and transforming the way we interact with our environment. However, with these exciting developments come concerns about data privacy, cybersecurity threats, and the widening digital divide. The need for ethical guidelines and regulations to govern the use of emerging technologies is more pressing than ever. As society becomes increasingly reliant on technology, it is crucial to anticipate the potential impact on individuals' mental health and social well-being. Striking a balance between embracing innovation and mitigating the negative consequences of technology will be essential for navigating the complex landscape of the digital age.

POTENTIAL SHIFTS IN SOCIETAL NORMS

The potential shifts in societal norms due to internet addiction are complex and multifaceted. As technology continues to advance at a rapid pace, individuals are becoming more reliant on digital devices for various aspects of their daily lives. This increasing dependence on technology has led to a shift in societal norms, with behaviors such as constant connectivity and the blurring of boundaries between work and personal life becoming more prevalent. Additionally, the rise of social media and online platforms has led to changes in how individuals communicate, socialize, and form relationships. These shifts in societal norms have significant implications for mental health, social interactions, and overall well-being. It is crucial for researchers, policymakers, and individuals alike to understand and address the impact of internet addiction on society in order to promote healthier and more balanced use of technology in today's digital age.

PREPARING FOR FUTURE CHALLENGES

Preparing for future challenges in combating internet addiction requires a multifaceted approach that involves collaboration among psychologists, educators, policymakers, and technology developers. One key aspect is enhancing digital literacy and promoting critical thinking skills among individuals, especially the youth, to empower them to make informed decisions regarding their online behaviors. Education programs should be implemented to raise awareness about the negative consequences of excessive internet use and provide strategies for responsible and balanced use of technology. Additionally, regulations and guidelines should be established to ensure that technology companies prioritize user well-being over profit. Research into the long-term effects of internet addiction and the development of effective interventions are also crucial in preparing for the challenges that may arise in the future. By taking proactive measures now, society can better mitigate the detrimental impacts of internet addiction and foster a healthier relationship with technology.

XXI. COMPARATIVE ANALYSIS OF INTERNET ADDICTION ACROSS CULTURES

Chapter XXI delves into the comparative analysis of internet addiction across different cultures, shedding light on the variations in prevalence and manifestations of this phenomenon. By examining how cultural factors such as values, norms, and social structures influence individuals' internet usage patterns and susceptibility to addiction, this research provides a comprehensive understanding of the complexities involved. The study reviews existing literature on internet addiction in diverse cultural contexts, identifying commonalities and differences that offer valuable insights for developing culturally sensitive prevention and intervention strategies. Through a nuanced exploration of the cultural nuances shaping internet addiction, this chapter contributes to the broader discourse on technology's impact on society. By recognizing the cultural diversity in experiences of internet addiction, researchers and practitioners can tailor approaches to address this issue effectively across various cultural settings.

CROSS-CULTURAL STUDIES ON INTERNET USAGE

Cross-cultural studies on internet usage have gained significant attention in recent years, shedding light on the diverse ways in which different cultures interact with and utilize the internet. These studies explore how cultural factors, such as individualism versus collectivism, impact online behaviors and attitudes. For instance, research has found that individualistic cultures may be more likely to use the internet for self-expression and personal branding, while collectivist cultures may prioritize social networking and community-building online. By examining these cross-cultural variations in internet usage, researchers can develop a more nuanced understanding of how technology intersects with cultural norms and values. This information is crucial for designing interventions and policies that are sensitive to the cultural context in which internet addiction and its consequences manifest. Ultimately, cross-cultural studies on internet usage offer valuable insights into the complex relationship between technology and society in a globalized world.

CULTURAL ATTITUDES TOWARDS TECHNOLOGY

Cultural attitudes towards technology play a pivotal role in shaping how individuals interact with and perceive the digital world. Some cultures embrace technological advancements, viewing them as opportunities for progress and innovation. These attitudes often lead to a high level of internet and technology usage in these societies. On the other hand, certain cultures may hold more conservative views towards technology, viewing it as a threat to traditional values and societal norms. This can lead to skepticism and resistance towards adopting new technologies. Understanding these cultural attitudes is crucial in addressing issues such as internet addiction, as different cultural perspectives can influence how individuals perceive and respond to technology-related problems. By recognizing and respecting diverse cultural attitudes towards technology, we can better navigate the challenges posed by excessive technology use in today's society.

GLOBAL VARIATIONS IN ADDICTION RATES

Global variations in addiction rates are a crucial aspect to consider when examining the impact of internet addiction on society. Research indicates that addiction rates vary significantly from country to country, influenced by cultural norms, socioeconomic factors, and access to technology. For instance, studies have shown that Asian countries tend to have higher rates of internet addiction compared to Western countries, possibly due to cultural factors that place a high emphasis on academic success and online gaming. Additionally, variations in internet addiction rates can also be seen within countries, with urban areas typically having higher rates compared to rural areas. Understanding these global variations in addiction rates is essential for developing targeted interventions and policies to address the growing issue of internet addiction and its detrimental effects on individuals and society.

XXII. THE NEUROSCIENCE OF INTERNET ADDICTION

The burgeoning issue of internet addiction has garnered significant attention in recent years, prompting researchers to delve into the neuroscience behind this growing phenomenon. Studies have shown that internet addiction activates similar neural pathways as substance abuse, particularly in the reward center of the brain. Neuroimaging techniques have revealed structural changes in the brains of individuals with internet addiction, such as reduced gray matter volume in areas responsible for cognitive control and decision-making. These alterations can lead to impaired impulse control and heightened cravings for online activities. Furthermore, neurotransmitter imbalances, specifically involving dopamine, have been implicated in the development and maintenance of internet addiction. Understanding the neurobiological mechanisms underlying this behavioral disorder is crucial for developing effective interventions and treatment strategies to mitigate its detrimental impact on individuals and society as a whole.

BRAIN CHANGES ASSOCIATED WITH ADDICTION

Brain changes associated with addiction are complex and multifaceted, involving alterations in the brain's reward system, executive functions, and stress response. Chronic exposure to addictive substances or behaviors leads to changes in neurotransmitter levels, particularly dopamine, which plays a crucial role in the reinforcement of addictive behaviors. These changes can result in a heightened sensitivity to drug-related cues, decreased sensitivity to natural rewards, and difficulty in inhibiting impulses, all of which contribute to the cycle of addiction. Additionally, addiction is associated with alterations in brain regions involved in decision making, such as the prefrontal cortex, leading to impaired judgment and decision-making abilities. Moreover, addiction can dysregulate the stress response system, leading to increased stress reactivity and a higher risk of relapse. Understanding these brain changes is crucial for developing effective interventions to combat addiction and mitigate its impact on individuals and society as a whole.

NEUROTRANSMITTERS AND REWARD PATHWAYS

Neurotransmitters play a crucial role in the reward pathways of the brain, which are closely linked to addictive behaviors such as internet addiction. The release of neurotransmitters such as dopamine, serotonin, and norepinephrine in response to pleasurable stimuli reinforces the behavior, leading to a cycle of craving and consumption. In the context of internet addiction, the continuous stimulation from engaging online activities can dysregulate these neurotransmitter systems, causing a heightened sensitivity to rewarding stimuli and a diminished response to natural rewards. This can result in compulsive behavior and a loss of control over internet usage. Understanding the neurobiological mechanisms underlying these reward pathways is essential for developing effective interventions to address internet addiction and its impact on individuals and society as a whole. By targeting neurotransmitter systems involved in reward processing, tailored treatments can be developed to address the complex nature of internet addiction.

COMPARISONS WITH OTHER FORMS OF ADDICTION

When exploring the phenomenon of Internet addiction, it is essential to consider how it compares to other forms of addiction. While traditional addiction models often focus on substances such as drugs or alcohol, Internet addiction presents unique challenges due to its pervasive nature in modern society. Unlike substance abuse, which is typically associated with physical dependence, Internet addiction revolves around psychological reliance on online activities. Studies have shown that individuals with Internet addiction exhibit similar brain patterns to those with substance use disorders, indicating underlying similarities in addictive behaviors. Furthermore, the ease of access to the Internet and the constant connectivity it provides can make managing Internet addiction particularly challenging. By examining these comparisons with other forms of addiction, we can gain a better understanding of the complexities of Internet addiction and its impact on society.

XXIII. THE ROLE OF PERSONALITY TRAITS IN INTERNET ADDICTION

Personality traits play a significant role in the development of Internet addiction, with various studies pointing to specific traits that are associated with an increased risk of developing problematic behaviors online. Extroversion, neuroticism, impulsivity, and sensation-seeking have all been linked to higher levels of Internet addiction, indicating that individuals with these traits may be more prone to excessive online use. These personality traits can influence how individuals interact with technology and the extent to which they seek gratification from online activities, potentially leading to addictive behaviors. Understanding the role of personality traits in Internet addiction is crucial for developing effective prevention and intervention strategies tailored to individual needs. By identifying individuals who may be at higher risk due to specific personality traits, researchers and clinicians can target interventions more effectively to address underlying psychological factors contributing to Internet addiction.

CORRELATION WITH INTROVERSION/EXTROVERSION

Research has shown a complex relationship between internet addiction and introversion/extroversion. Introverted individuals may be more susceptible to internet addiction due to the anonymity and reduced social interaction that online platforms provide, offering a sense of escape from real-life social situations. On the other hand, extroverts may use the internet as a tool for socializing and networking, leading to increased usage but not necessarily addiction. This correlation highlights the importance of considering personality traits when studying internet addiction and its impact on individuals. Understanding how introversion/extroversion interacts with internet use can provide insights into the underlying motivations and behaviors that contribute to addiction. By recognizing these differences, interventions and prevention strategies can be tailored to address the specific needs of individuals based on their personality traits and tendencies towards internet use.

IMPULSIVITY AND RISK-TAKING BEHAVIORS

Impulsivity and risk-taking behaviors are often intertwined, particularly in the realm of technology use. Individuals who exhibit high levels of impulsivity may be more prone to engaging in risky online activities, such as cyberbullying, online gambling, or sharing personal information with strangers. This behavior can have significant consequences, both personally and socially. For example, individuals who impulsively share sensitive information online may become victims of identity theft, while those who engage in cyberbullying may face legal repercussions. Understanding the relationship between impulsivity and risk-taking behaviors in the context of technology is crucial for developing effective interventions and prevention strategies. By addressing underlying impulsivity issues and promoting responsible online behavior, we can mitigate the negative impact of internet addiction on today's society. This research aims to explore these complex dynamics and provide valuable insights for both academics and practitioners in the field.

SELF-ESTEEM AND VALIDATION-SEEKING

Self-esteem plays a crucial role in individuals' propensity for internet addiction. Those with low self-esteem often turn to the internet for validation and reassurance, seeking likes, comments, and followers to boost their self-worth. This constant need for external validation can lead to a vicious cycle of dependency on social media platforms to feel accepted and validated. However, this reliance on digital affirmation can have detrimental effects on mental health and self-esteem in the long run. As individuals become more addicted to seeking validation online, they may neglect real-life relationships and opportunities for genuine self-improvement. It is essential for researchers and psychologists to further explore the link between self-esteem and validation-seeking behaviors in the context of internet addiction to develop effective interventions and strategies for individuals at risk.

XXIV. THE IMPACT OF INTERNET ADDICTION ON CREATIVITY

Internet addiction has become a prevalent issue in today's society, with individuals spending increasing amounts of time online, often to the detriment of their mental health and overall well-being. One concerning aspect of internet addiction is its potential impact on creativity. Research suggests that excessive use of the internet can hinder creative thinking and problem-solving skills, as individuals become more reliant on instant information and lose the ability to think critically and creatively. This reliance on the internet for constant stimulation and gratification can inhibit the development of innovative ideas and original thought processes. As a result, individuals may struggle to think outside the box and come up with novel solutions to complex problems. Addressing internet addiction and promoting mindful internet use is crucial to preserving and enhancing creativity in today's digital age.

INFLUENCE ON ARTISTIC AND CREATIVE PURSUITS

Artistic and creative pursuits have been significantly influenced by technology, particularly the internet, in today's society. The ease of access to a plethora of resources and inspiration online has revolutionized the way artists and creatives work and collaborate. Platforms like social media have provided artists with a global audience and the ability to showcase their work to a larger demographic. Additionally, the internet has made it possible for individuals to learn new techniques and skills through online courses and tutorials, empowering more people to pursue artistic endeavors. However, the constant connectivity and distractions offered by the internet can also become a hindrance to creativity, leading to potential internet addiction and a lack of focus on one's artistic pursuits. As technology continues to evolve, it is crucial for individuals to find a balance between utilizing its benefits for creativity while also maintaining a healthy relationship with the digital world.

THE DISTRACTIVE NATURE OF THE INTERNET ON CREATIVITY

The widespread use of the internet has undeniably revolution-ized the way we access information and communicate with oth-ers. However, this constant connectivity comes with its draw-backs, particularly in the realm of creativity. The internet's vast amount of distractions, from social media notifications to end-less browsing options, can easily derail individuals from focusing on their creative pursuits. Research shows that excessive inter-net use can lead to feelings of overwhelm and mental fatigue, ultimately hindering the creative process. In a society that val-ues productivity and instant gratification, the allure of the inter-net's distractions can be difficult to resist. As such, it is crucial for individuals to be mindful of their internet usage and imple-ment strategies to cultivate focused and uninterrupted creative time. By acknowledging the distractive nature of the internet and taking proactive steps to mitigate its influence, individuals can tap into their full creative potential and produce meaningful, original work.

OPPORTUNITIES FOR CREATIVE EXPRESSION ONLINE

In the realm of online activities, the internet provides a vast array of opportunities for creative expression. From personal blogs and social media platforms to digital art and online gaming, individuals have the freedom to express themselves in diverse and innovative ways. The online environment allows for the exploration of different identities, fostering a sense of empowerment and self-discovery. Through the creation of digital content, individuals can engage with a global audience and cultivate a community around shared interests. This interconnectedness promotes collaboration and the exchange of ideas, leading to the emergence of new forms of artistic expression. However, while the internet offers avenues for creativity and self-expression, it is essential to consider the potential risks and challenges associated with online activities, such as privacy concerns and exposure to harmful content. As society continues to navigate the complexities of the digital age, it is crucial to strike a balance between embracing the opportunities for creative expression online and safeguarding against potential pitfalls.

XXV. INTERNET ADDICTION AND CONSUMER BEHAVIOR

The rise of Internet addiction has become a significant concern in today's society, impacting consumer behavior in various ways. As individuals increasingly spend more time online, they are exposed to a multitude of advertisements, promotions, and consumer reviews, shaping their purchasing decisions. Moreover, the convenience and ease of online shopping have led to impulsive buying behaviors, contributing to the phenomenon of compulsive buying among Internet addicts. On the other hand, excessive time spent online can also lead to information overload and decision fatigue, resulting in consumers making poor choices or being unable to make a decision at all. As researchers delve deeper into the complex relationship between Internet addiction and consumer behavior, it is crucial to consider the implications of this issue on individuals' well-being and the economy as a whole. By addressing the underlying factors driving Internet addiction and its impact on consumer behavior, we can develop strategies to mitigate its negative consequences and promote healthier online habits.

ONLINE SHOPPING AND IMPULSE BUYING

Online shopping has rapidly become a dominant mode of consumption, offering convenience and accessibility to consumers around the globe. However, this convenience has also paved the way for impulse buying, a phenomenon fueled by the instant gratification and easy access to an abundance of products online. The allure of one-click purchasing and targeted advertisements can lead individuals to make impulsive and often unnecessary purchases. From a psychological perspective, the lack of physical barriers and time constraints in online shopping can lower inhibitions and increase the likelihood of impulse buying. Understanding the factors that contribute to online impulse buying is essential in addressing the negative consequences such as financial strain and cluttered living spaces. As technology continues to advance, strategies must be developed to mitigate the impact of online shopping on impulsive purchasing behavior.

INFLUENCE OF DIGITAL MARKETING

In today's digital age, the influence of digital marketing has become increasingly pervasive, shaping consumer behavior and driving industry trends. The rise of social media platforms and online advertising has revolutionized the way businesses engage with their target audience, allowing for personalized and targeted marketing strategies. However, the proliferation of digital marketing techniques has also raised concerns about privacy, data security, and the potential for manipulation. By utilizing sophisticated algorithms and tracking tools, companies can collect vast amounts of personal data to tailor their marketing efforts. This practice has sparked debates about the ethical implications of digital marketing and the need for regulation to safeguard consumer rights. As technology continues to advance, it is crucial for researchers to explore the double-edged sword of digital marketing, recognizing its potential benefits while also addressing its drawbacks and implications for society as a whole.

CONSUMER DATA AND TARGETED ADVERTISING

Consumer data and targeted advertising have become increasingly intertwined due to the advancement of technology. In today's digital landscape, companies have access to vast amounts of personal information, allowing them to tailor their marketing strategies to specific demographics with unprecedented precision. While this may lead to more relevant and personalized advertising for consumers, it also raises concerns about privacy and data security. The practice of targeted advertising has the potential to manipulate consumer behavior and perpetuate a cycle of constant consumption. Moreover, the collection and use of consumer data without explicit consent can infringe upon individual rights and autonomy. As technology continues to evolve, it is crucial for regulators and policymakers to establish strict guidelines to protect consumer data and ensure transparent practices in targeted advertising. This balance between personalized marketing and consumer privacy will be a key challenge in shaping the future of the digital economy.

XXVI. THE INTERSECTION OF INTERNET ADDICTION AND CYBERSECURITY

The intersection of internet addiction and cybersecurity presents a complex challenge in today's digital age. On one hand, individuals who are addicted to the internet may be more susceptible to cyber threats due to their excessive online presence and risky behaviors. Their compulsive need to constantly check social media, play online games, or shop online can expose them to various online scams, phishing attacks, and malware. On the other hand, cyber criminals may exploit vulnerable individuals with internet addiction by targeting them with tailored scams or malware designed to take advantage of their compulsive online habits. Therefore, it is crucial for cybersecurity professionals to not only focus on technical solutions but also consider the psychological aspects of internet addiction when developing strategies to protect individuals from online threats. By understanding the intersection between internet addiction and cybersecurity, we can develop more holistic approaches to address the risks associated with excessive internet usage in today's society.

RISKS OF COMPULSIVE ONLINE BEHAVIORS

The risks associated with compulsive online behaviors are multifaceted and complex, stemming from a variety of factors such as psychological, social, and physiological dimensions. Individuals who engage in excessive internet use may face adverse consequences on their mental health, including increased levels of stress, anxiety, and depression. Moreover, compulsive online behaviors can lead to a decline in academic or occupational performance, as individuals may prioritize online activities over their responsibilities and obligations. In addition, excessive screen time can have detrimental effects on physical health, contributing to sedentary lifestyles and related health problems. Furthermore, compulsive online behaviors may also disrupt personal relationships and social interactions, as individuals may struggle to connect with others in the real world. Understanding the risks associated with compulsive online behaviors is crucial in developing interventions and strategies to address internet addiction and its impact on individuals and society as a whole.

114

PROTECTING PERSONAL INFORMATION

Protecting personal information is crucial in today's digital age, where data breaches and identity theft are rampant. It is imperative for individuals to take proactive steps to safeguard their sensitive information, such as using strong passwords, enabling two-factor authentication, and being cautious about sharing personal details online. Furthermore, companies and organizations must prioritize data security by implementing robust encryption protocols, regularly updating their cybersecurity measures, and providing adequate training to employees on handling sensitive information. Government regulations and policies also play a significant role in protecting personal data, ensuring that companies adhere to strict standards and face consequences for breaches. By collectively taking these measures, we can help mitigate the risks associated with internet addiction and safeguard our personal information in an increasingly interconnected world.

THE ROLE OF USER AWARENESS IN CYBERSECURITY

User awareness plays a crucial role in cybersecurity, especially as technology continues to advance rapidly. Educating users about the importance of strong passwords, recognizing phishing attempts, and understanding the risks of sharing personal information online is essential in preventing cyber-attacks. A lack of user awareness can leave individuals and organizations vulnerable to various cyber threats, ultimately compromising sensitive data and financial resources. By promoting a culture of cybersecurity awareness, users can become more proactive in safeguarding their online activities and information. Training programs, workshops, and regular updates on emerging cyber threats are effective strategies to enhance user awareness and foster a sense of responsibility in maintaining a secure online environment. Ultimately, user awareness serves as a frontline defense in the ever-evolving landscape of cybersecurity, mitigating risks and protecting against potential cyber threats.

XXVII. THE INFLUENCE OF INTERNET ADDICTION ON LANGUAGE AND COMMUNICATION

Examining the impact of internet addiction on language and communication reveals a complex relationship between technology and human interaction. As individuals spend increasing amounts of time online, their communication skills may be affected by the prevalence of digital platforms. The use of abbreviations, emojis, and informal language in online communication can lead to a decline in formal writing and speaking abilities. Moreover, excessive use of the internet can isolate individuals, reducing their opportunities for face-to-face communication and social interaction. This shift towards digital communication may result in a loss of nuance and depth in interpersonal relationships. Understanding the effects of internet addiction on language and communication is crucial in order to address the challenges posed by this modern phenomenon and to promote effective communication in today's society.

EVOLUTION OF ONLINE COMMUNICATION STYLES

The evolution of online communication styles has played a significant role in shaping the way individuals interact in today's society. With the advancement of technology and the rise of social media platforms, there has been a shift towards more informal and concise communication methods. This has led to the development of new norms and etiquette in online interactions, challenging traditional forms of communication. The widespread use of emojis, acronyms, and gifs has changed the way messages are conveyed and interpreted, affecting the overall tone and meaning of conversations. However, this shift has also raised concerns about the impact on language skills and the quality of communication. As individuals continue to adapt to these new styles of online communication, it is essential to consider the implications for social interactions and interpersonal relationships. Understanding the evolution of online communication styles is crucial in comprehending the broader effects of technology on society.

IMPACT ON LINGUISTIC SKILLS

The impact of technology on linguistic skills is a topic of great importance in today's society, particularly concerning the rise of internet addiction. Research has shown that excessive use of technology, such as smartphones and social media, can have detrimental effects on language development and communication abilities. Users may rely on shortcuts like emojis and acronyms, leading to a decrease in proficiency in traditional forms of communication. Additionally, the constant barrage of information from the internet can overwhelm the brain's processing capacity, making it harder for individuals to concentrate and retain information. These challenges can hinder linguistic skills, including vocabulary acquisition, grammar proficiency, and overall communication effectiveness. As such, it is crucial for researchers and policymakers to address the negative impact of technology on linguistic abilities and consider strategies to mitigate these effects in today's society.

THE ROLE OF EMOJIS AND INTERNET SLANG

In the realm of internet communication, emojis and internet slang play a significant role in shaping the way individuals interact online. Emojis, with their ability to convey emotions and tone in a concise manner, have become a popular communication tool, particularly among younger generations. They add depth and nuance to written messages, helping to bridge the gap created by the absence of nonverbal cues in digital communication. On the other hand, internet slang, characterized by abbreviations, acronyms, and unconventional spellings, serves as a form of linguistic creativity and expression. It allows for efficient communication in a fast-paced online environment while fostering a sense of community among users who share common slang. However, the excessive use of emojis and internet slang can lead to misinterpretations, misunderstandings, and the erosion of traditional language norms. It is essential to strike a balance between leveraging these tools for efficient communication and preserving the richness of language in the digital age.

XXVIII. INTERNET ADDICTION AND ENVIRONMENTAL CONCERNS

Internet addiction is a growing concern in contemporary society, with individuals becoming increasingly reliant on digital technologies for their daily activities. This addiction not only affects individuals' mental and physical health but also has broader environmental implications. The excessive use of electronic devices leads to increased energy consumption, contributing to carbon emissions and environmental degradation. Moreover, the production, disposal, and recycling of electronic devices generate electronic waste that further pollutes the environment. As society becomes more technology-dependent, it is crucial to recognize the interconnectedness between internet addiction and environmental concerns. Sustainable practices, such as reducing energy consumption, promoting electronic recycling, and raising awareness about the environmental impacts of technology addiction, are essential in mitigating the detrimental effects on both individuals and the environment. By addressing internet addiction, we can also work towards creating a more sustainable and environmentally conscious society.

DIGITAL CARBON FOOTPRINT

One crucial aspect of technological advancement that has gained increasing attention in recent years is the concept of a digital carbon footprint. As industries and individuals rely more on digital devices and services, the environmental impact of these digital activities cannot be ignored. The production and disposal of electronic devices, as well as the energy consumption associated with data storage and transmission, all contribute to the carbon footprint of the digital world. Understanding and mitigating this footprint is essential for sustainable development and environmental conservation. Researchers and policymakers need to consider the environmental consequences of our digital lifestyles and work towards implementing strategies to minimize the carbon footprint of the digital era. By raising awareness and promoting eco-friendly practices in the digital realm, we can strive towards a more sustainable future for our planet.

E-WASTE AND RECYCLING CHALLENGES

E-waste poses a significant challenge for society as technology advances at a rapid pace, leading to the constant upgrading and discarding of electronic devices. The disposal of e-waste presents environmental and health hazards due to toxic components such as lead, mercury, and arsenic. Recycling e-waste is crucial to mitigate these risks, but this process is complicated by the intricate composition of electronic devices. Separating valuable materials from electronic waste requires specialized equipment and processes, making recycling both costly and resource-intensive. Moreover, ineffective collection and disorganized recycling systems in many countries contribute to the global e-waste problem. Addressing these challenges necessitates a concerted effort from manufacturers, policymakers, and consumers to implement sustainable e-waste management practices and promote circular economy principles in the electronics industry.

ENERGY CONSUMPTION OF DIGITAL INFRASTRUCTURE

The energy consumption of digital infrastructure is a critical issue that needs to be addressed in today's society. As technology continues to advance, the demand for digital services and online platforms increases, leading to a significant rise in energy consumption. The environmental impact of this energy usage cannot be ignored, as the reliance on fossil fuels for power generation contributes to greenhouse gas emissions and climate change. It is essential for researchers and policymakers to find sustainable solutions to reduce the energy consumption of digital infrastructure while still meeting the increasing demand for digital services. This may involve investing in renewable energy sources, improving energy efficiency in data centers, and promoting responsible consumption habits among individuals. By addressing the energy consumption of digital infrastructure, we can mitigate the environmental impact of technology and work towards a more sustainable future.

XXIX. THE ROLE OF ARTIFICIAL INTELLIGENCE IN INTERNET ADDICTION

Recent advancements in artificial intelligence have introduced new challenges in the realm of internet addiction. AI algorithms are increasingly being used by tech companies to personalize content, enhance user engagement, and increase platform retention. These AI-driven features are tailored to exploit psychological vulnerabilities, leading to addictive behavior patterns in users. Furthermore, AI-powered recommendation systems often create filter bubbles, enhancing echo chambers and reinforcing addictive browsing habits. On the flip side, artificial intelligence also holds promise in mitigating internet addiction by developing algorithms that can track and manage online behaviors, providing personalized interventions and nudges to limit excessive usage. However, the ethical implications of AI surveillance and intervention in individuals' online activities must be carefully considered to avoid potential privacy infringements and unintended consequences. As we navigate the complex interplay between AI technology and internet addiction, it is imperative to strike a balance between harnessing AI for positive interventions while safeguarding against its potential for exacerbating addictive behaviors.

AI IN CURATING ONLINE CONTENT

AI in curating online content has become a prevalent practice in today's digital landscape. As advancements in artificial intelligence technology continue to progress, the capabilities of AI in sorting and delivering online information have expanded. AI algorithms can analyze vast amounts of data in real-time, allowing for more personalized and relevant content recommendations for users. However, the use of AI in curating online content raises concerns regarding privacy, data security, and ethical considerations. Issues such as filter bubbles, where algorithms only show users content that aligns with their existing beliefs, can contribute to the spread of misinformation and polarize online communities. Therefore, while AI can enhance user experiences by tailoring content to individual preferences, it is crucial to address the potential negative impacts and implications of relying solely on AI algorithms for content curation in order to maintain a balanced and diverse online environment.

AI AND PERSONALIZATION OF USER EXPERIENCE

AI has revolutionized the personalization of user experiences on digital platforms. By analyzing vast amounts of data, AI algorithms can predict user preferences and behaviors, leading to tailored recommendations and content delivery. This level of customization enhances user engagement and satisfaction, ultimately driving business growth. However, the extensive use of AI in personalization can also have negative implications. Over-reliance on algorithmic recommendations may result in filter bubbles, where users are only exposed to information that aligns with their existing beliefs, reinforcing echo chambers and limiting exposure to diverse perspectives. Additionally, concerns surrounding data privacy and security arise as AI systems collect and analyze personal information to personalize experiences. Striking a balance between personalization and privacy is crucial in navigating the double-edged sword of AI in user experience customization.

ETHICAL CONSIDERATIONS OF AI IN USER ENGAGEMENT

Ethical considerations surrounding the use of AI in user engagement are crucial in the context of technological advancements and their impact on society. AI has the potential to greatly enhance user experiences by personalizing interactions and predicting user needs. However, the collection and utilization of vast amounts of user data raise concerns about privacy, security, and potential misuse of information. The ethical implications of AI algorithms making decisions on behalf of users and influencing behavior also come into play. Stakeholders must prioritize transparency, accountability, and user consent in the development and deployment of AI systems. Moreover, ensuring fairness and non-discrimination in AI applications is essential to uphold ethical standards. By addressing these ethical considerations thoughtfully and proactively, researchers and practitioners can harness the benefits of AI while mitigating potential harms to individuals and society as a whole.

XXX. THE DICHOTOMY OF CONNECTIVITY AND ISOLATION

The dichotomy of connectivity and isolation is a complex issue that plagues modern society, particularly in the realm of technology. On one hand, advancements in technology have brought unprecedented levels of connectivity, allowing individuals to communicate and collaborate with others across the globe instantaneously. This interconnectedness has revolutionized the way we work, socialize, and access information. However, the flip side of this connectivity is a growing sense of isolation and disconnection from the physical world. The constant barrage of notifications, messages, and social media interactions can lead to a sense of overwhelm and alienation from real-life relationships and experiences. As we become increasingly reliant on digital devices for communication and entertainment, the line between genuine human connection and virtual interaction becomes blurred. It is crucial for society to strike a balance between utilizing technology for connectivity while also fostering meaningful face-to-face connections to combat the pervasive feelings of isolation that technology can exacerbate.

THE ILLUSION OF BEING CONNECTED

One of the paradoxes of the digital age is the illusion of being connected that technology creates. While we are constantly surrounded by screens and notifications, the quality of our connections may be superficial and lacking in depth. This illusion of connection can lead to isolation and alienation, as real human interaction is replaced by virtual exchanges. Individuals may spend hours scrolling through social media feeds, yet still feel disconnected and lonely. This phenomenon highlights the double-sided nature of technology, where the promise of connection can paradoxically result in disconnection. Understanding the impact of this illusion on mental health and social relationships is crucial in addressing the prevalence of internet addiction in today's society. By examining the underlying factors that contribute to this illusion, we can develop strategies to foster genuine connections and combat the negative effects of excessive screen time.

THE REALITY OF SOCIAL ISOLATION

Social isolation is a growing concern in today's society, exacerbated by the prevalence of technology and internet addiction. The reality of social isolation is a complex phenomenon that can have serious implications on an individual's mental health and well-being. Research has shown that prolonged periods of isolation can lead to increased feelings of loneliness, depression, and anxiety. Moreover, social isolation has been linked to a range of physical health issues, including high blood pressure, cardiovascular disease, and even a weakened immune system. In the context of internet addiction, individuals may be more prone to withdrawing from face-to-face interactions, further isolating themselves in the digital world. As such, it is crucial for researchers and policymakers to address the reality of social isolation and its impact on individuals in today's interconnected yet socially fragmented society.

FINDING BALANCE IN A DIGITALLY CONNECTED WORLD

Finding balance in a digitally connected world has become increasingly challenging as technology continues to advance at a rapid pace. The allure of constant connectivity and instant gratification can lead to a myriad of negative effects on individuals' well-being, such as Internet addiction. This pervasive issue is characterized by excessive use of technology, leading to neglect of real-life interactions and responsibilities. However, it is essential to acknowledge that technology also brings numerous benefits, such as increased efficiency and connectivity. Striking a balance between utilizing technology for its advantages while also maintaining boundaries to prevent addiction is crucial. By practicing mindfulness, setting limits on screen time, and prioritizing face-to-face interactions, individuals can cultivate a healthier relationship with technology. Ultimately, finding this equilibrium in a digitally connected world is paramount for maintaining mental and emotional well-being in today's society.

XXXI. THE IMPACT OF INTERNET ADDICTION ON SLEEP PATTERNS

The prevalence of internet addiction has become a growing concern in today's society, with individuals spending increasing amounts of time online. One area that has been significantly affected by this phenomenon is sleep patterns. Research has shown that individuals who are addicted to the internet often experience disrupted sleep, leading to a range of negative consequences on their health and well-being. The excessive use of electronic devices before bedtime can interfere with the production of melatonin, a hormone that regulates sleep, resulting in difficulties falling asleep and poor sleep quality. Moreover, the constant access to the internet can lead to individuals staying up late into the night, engaging in online activities, and subsequently experiencing sleep deprivation. This cycle of internet addiction and disrupted sleep patterns can have detrimental effects on cognitive functions, mood regulation, and overall quality of life. As such, it is crucial to address the impact of internet addiction on sleep patterns to promote healthy and balanced use of technology in today's society.

BLUE LIGHT EXPOSURE AND CIRCADIAN RHYTHMS

Blue light exposure has been found to have a significant impact on circadian rhythms, which are crucial for maintaining a healthy sleep-wake cycle. Studies have shown that exposure to blue light, particularly from electronic devices such as smartphones and laptops, can disrupt the production of melatonin, the hormone responsible for regulating sleep. This disruption can lead to difficulty falling asleep and result in poor sleep quality. As technology continues to advance and become increasingly integrated into daily life, the prevalence of blue light exposure has also increased. It is important for individuals to be mindful of the potential effects of blue light exposure on their circadian rhythms and take steps to mitigate these impacts, such as using blue light filters on devices or limiting screen time before bedtime. By understanding the relationship between blue light exposure and circadian rhythms, individuals can make informed decisions about their technology use to prioritize their overall health and well-being.

SLEEP QUALITY AND INTERNET USE BEFORE BEDTIME

Research has shown a significant association between poor sleep quality and excessive internet use before bedtime. The blue light emitted by screens can disrupt the production of melatonin, a hormone that regulates sleep-wake cycles, leading to difficulty falling asleep and reduced sleep duration. Furthermore, engaging in stimulating online activities can activate the brain and increase alertness, making it harder to relax and unwind before bed. This can result in a vicious cycle of using the internet to wind down, which in turn disrupts sleep and leads to the reliance on more screen time to combat fatigue. As technology continues to advance and become more integrated into daily life, it is crucial to examine the impact of internet use on sleep quality and consider interventions to promote healthier bedtime routines. By addressing this issue, individuals can improve their overall well-being and productivity in today's tech-driven society.

STRATEGIES FOR IMPROVING SLEEP HYGIENE

Strategies for improving sleep hygiene among individuals struggling with internet addiction are essential in mitigating the detrimental impact on their overall well-being. One effective approach is establishing a consistent sleep routine, where bedtime
and wake-up times are fixed to regulate the body's internal
clock. Additionally, creating a comfortable sleep environment
free of electronic devices can promote relaxation and improve
sleep quality. Cognitive-behavioral therapy has also shown
promise in addressing sleep disturbances associated with technology overuse by identifying and modifying negative thought
patterns that contribute to insomnia. Moreover, incorporating
relaxation techniques such as mindfulness meditation or pro-
gressive muscle relaxation can help reduce stress and improve
the ability to fall asleep. By implementing these strategies, individuals can enhance their sleep hygiene, leading to better
mental health outcomes and a reduced risk of internet addic-
tion-related issues.

XXXII. THE ROLE OF INTERNET ADDICTION IN MODERN PARENTING

In modern parenting, the role of internet addiction has become a pressing concern. As parents increasingly rely on digital devices for entertainment, communication, and information, the risk of developing unhealthy behaviors around screen time has grown. Children are particularly vulnerable to the allure of the internet, with studies showing that excessive use can lead to social isolation, poor academic performance, and even mental health issues. As such, parents must be vigilant in monitoring their children's online activities and setting limits to prevent the negative consequences of internet addiction. However, it is also important to acknowledge the positive aspects of technology in education and social connection. Finding a balance between the benefits and risks of internet use is crucial for effective parenting in the digital age. By promoting responsible digital behavior and modeling healthy habits, parents can empower their children to navigate the online world safely and responsibly.

PARENTAL CONTROLS AND MONITORING

Parental controls and monitoring play a crucial role in addressing the issue of internet addiction and its impact on today's society. By using parental control tools, parents can restrict access to certain websites and content that may contribute to addictive behaviors. Monitoring software can also provide insights into a child's online activities, allowing parents to identify potential warning signs of addiction early on. However, it is essential for parents to strike a balance between monitoring and invading their child's privacy, as excessive control may lead to feelings of distrust and rebellion. Therefore, a collaborative approach between parents and children, involving open communication and setting boundaries together, is key to effectively using parental controls and monitoring to combat internet addiction. Ultimately, these tools should be seen as a means to promote healthy and responsible digital habits rather than as a strict form of surveillance.

MODELING HEALTHY INTERNET USE FOR CHILDREN

Modeling healthy internet use for children is crucial in today's digital age. Parents, educators, and policymakers play a significant role in shaping children's online behaviors. By setting clear boundaries, monitoring screen time, and promoting offline activities, adults can instill good internet habits in young individuals. Moreover, fostering open communication about online experiences and potential dangers can help children navigate the virtual world safely. Providing positive role models and engaging in joint online activities can also promote healthy internet use. Educational programs focusing on digital literacy and cyber safety are essential for equipping children with the necessary skills to navigate the ever-evolving online landscape. By promoting responsible internet use from a young age, we can help mitigate the risks of internet addiction and ensure that children develop into well-rounded individuals in today's society.

THE CHALLENGE OF SCREEN TIME FOR KIDS

Screen time for children has become a pressing issue in today's technology-driven society. The challenge lies in finding a balance between the benefits of digital devices for educational and entertainment purposes and the potential harmful effects of excessive screen time on children's development. Research indicates that excessive screen time may contribute to issues such as obesity, poor sleep quality, and psychological problems. Parents and caregivers face the difficult task of navigating the digital landscape and setting appropriate limits on screen time for their children. Strategies such as setting boundaries, engaging in alternative activities, and promoting outdoor play can help mitigate the negative impact of excessive screen time. By addressing the challenge of screen time for kids thoughtfully and proactively, we can better support the well-being and healthy development of the younger generation in the digital age.

XXXIII. THE INFLUENCE OF INTERNET ADDICTION ON BODY IMAGE AND SELF-PERCEPTION

The impact of internet addiction on body image and self-perception is a crucial aspect of modern society that needs to be carefully examined. Individuals who spend excessive amounts of time online may be exposed to unrealistic beauty standards and filtered representations of reality, leading to negative comparisons and feelings of inadequacy. This can result in a distorted self-perception and unhealthy body image, ultimately affecting mental health and well-being. Research has shown that those who struggle with internet addiction may engage in compulsive behaviors such as constant selfies, editing photos, and seeking validation through likes and comments. It is essential for society to recognize the detrimental effects of internet addiction on body image and self-perception in order to promote a healthier relationship with technology and oneself. By raising awareness and implementing strategies to manage internet use, individuals can work towards cultivating a positive self-image and improved mental health outcomes.

SOCIAL MEDIA AND BODY IMAGE CONCERNS

Social media has become a prominent platform for individuals to showcase themselves online, leading to concerns about body image. Studies have shown a correlation between social media usage and increased body dissatisfaction, particularly among younger generations who are exposed to unrealistic beauty standards online. The constant comparison to edited and filtered images on social media can contribute to low self-esteem and poor body image. In addition, the pressure to attain the "perfect" body as portrayed on social media can lead to disordered eating behaviors and other mental health issues. It is crucial for researchers and mental health professionals to address the negative impact of social media on body image concerns and promote body positivity and self-acceptance in the digital age. By understanding the complex relationship between social media and body image, interventions can be developed to help individuals navigate these challenges and foster a healthier relationship with their bodies.

ONLINE COMPARISON AND SELF-ESTEEM

The proliferation of social media platforms and online comparison has been linked to changes in individuals' self-esteem. The constant exposure to curated and often idealized versions of others' lives on social media can lead to feelings of inadequacy and lower self-worth. Studies have shown that individuals who engage frequently in online comparison are more likely to experience negative psychological outcomes, such as anxiety and depression. On the other hand, some research also suggests that online comparison can serve as a source of motivation for self-improvement and goal setting. It is crucial for researchers and practitioners to understand the complexities of how online comparison impacts self-esteem and develop strategies to mitigate its negative effects while harnessing its potential benefits for personal growth and well-being in today's digitally connected society.

PROMOTING POSITIVE SELF-IMAGE IN THE DIGITAL AGE

In the digital age, promoting positive self-image has become increasingly important as individuals are bombarded with unrealistic beauty standards and cyberbullying through social media platforms. To address this issue, it is vital to implement interventions that focus on fostering self-esteem, self-compassion, and resilience among individuals, especially young people who are more vulnerable to the negative impacts of social media. Education and awareness campaigns can play a crucial role in helping individuals navigate the online world and develop a healthy relationship with technology. Additionally, creating safe spaces online where individuals can freely express themselves without fear of judgment or criticism can greatly contribute to promoting positive self-image. By advocating for self-acceptance and promoting authenticity in the digital realm, we can work towards creating a more supportive and empowering online environment for all individuals.

XXXIV. THE RELATIONSHIP BETWEEN INTERNET ADDICTION AND JOB SATISFACTION

The impact of internet addiction on job satisfaction is a topic that has garnered increased attention in recent years. Studies have shown that individuals who exhibit signs of internet addiction, such as excessive use of social media or online gaming, are more likely to experience lower levels of job satisfaction. This may be attributed to the negative consequences of internet addiction on productivity, focus, and overall well-being in the workplace. Moreover, employees who are constantly engaged in online activities may struggle to maintain a healthy work-life balance, leading to feelings of burnout and dissatisfaction with their job roles. It is crucial for organizations to address the issue of internet addiction among employees, implementing strategies to promote healthy internet usage and create a supportive work environment that prioritizes employee well-being. By recognizing the link between internet addiction and job satisfaction, employers can take proactive measures to improve workplace satisfaction and overall productivity.

ONLINE DISTRACTIONS AND WORK ENGAGEMENT

There is a growing concern about the impact of online distractions on work engagement in today's society. While the internet has provided countless benefits for productivity and communication, it also poses a significant threat to individuals' ability to stay focused and engaged in their work. Recent studies have shown that constant access to social media, email, and other online platforms can lead to decreased attention span, increased procrastination, and overall reduced work performance. This issue is further compounded by the addictive nature of digital devices, which can make it challenging for individuals to disconnect and fully immerse themselves in their tasks. Therefore, it is crucial for organizations to implement strategies to help employees manage online distractions effectively, such as setting boundaries on technology use during work hours and promoting mindfulness practices to improve focus and concentration. Ultimately, finding a balance between technology use and work engagement is essential for maintaining productivity and well-being in the digital age.

TELECOMMUTING AND THE BLURRING OF WORK-LIFE BOUNDARIES

Telecommuting has become increasingly prevalent in today's workforce, with advancements in technology allowing for remote work opportunities. While this offers flexibility and convenience, it also blurs the boundaries between work and personal life. The accessibility of work email and communication tools means employees may find it challenging to disconnect from work, leading to increased stress and burnout. Moreover, the lack of physical separation between home and office can disrupt work-life balance, making it harder for individuals to fully engage in personal activities and recharge. As a result, it is crucial for organizations to establish clear policies and boundaries around telecommuting to ensure employees can effectively manage their time and maintain a healthy work-life balance. By addressing these challenges, telecommuting can be a beneficial arrangement that promotes productivity and employee well-being.

STRATEGIES FOR MAINTAINING JOB SATISFACTION IN THE DIGITAL ERA

In the digital era, strategies for maintaining job satisfaction have become increasingly important as technological advancements continue to reshape the workplace. One key strategy is to prioritize work-life balance by setting boundaries between work and personal time, utilizing technology to increase efficiency rather than allowing it to blur the lines between work and leisure. Another effective approach is for organizations to provide opportunities for professional development and growth, such as offering training programs to help employees stay up-to-date with digital skills. Additionally, fostering a culture of open communication and feedback can enhance employee engagement and job satisfaction. By implementing these strategies, individuals and organizations can navigate the complexities of the digital age and promote a positive work environment conducive to job satisfaction and overall well-being.

XXXV. THE ROLE OF INTERNET ADDICTION IN EMERGENCY AND CRISIS SITUATIONS

In emergency and crisis situations, the role of internet addiction can have both positive and negative impacts. On one hand, the internet can serve as a valuable tool for communication, coordination, and disseminating critical information during times of crisis. Individuals who are addicted to the internet may use their excessive online presence to stay informed, connect with loved ones, and seek help when needed. However, the detrimental effects of internet addiction cannot be overlooked. Those who are compulsively drawn to the internet may neglect real-life responsibilities, fail to respond efficiently in emergency situations, and prioritize their online activities over actual emergencies. This lack of presence and focus can hinder effective decision-making and response efforts in times of crisis. As such, it is crucial to recognize and address the impact of internet addiction in emergency situations to ensure the well-being and safety of individuals and communities.

INFORMATION DISSEMINATION DURING CRISES

Information dissemination during crises is a crucial aspect of managing emergency situations. In today's technologically advanced society, the internet plays a significant role in how information is distributed during times of crisis. Social media platforms, websites, and mobile apps serve as vital tools for rapid communication and updates. However, the overwhelming amount of information available online can also lead to misinformation and confusion. It is essential for government agencies, organizations, and individuals to be able to discern credible sources from false information to prevent panic and ensure public safety. Furthermore, the speed at which information spreads on the internet can either alleviate or exacerbate a crisis situation, depending on the accuracy and timeliness of the information shared. Therefore, developing strategies for effective information dissemination online is paramount in today's digital age to mitigate the negative impacts of misinformation during emergencies.

THE SPREAD OF MISINFORMATION AND PANIC

The spread of misinformation and panic in today's society is a concerning issue exacerbated by the rapid dissemination of information through technology. With the rise of social media platforms and instant messaging applications, false information can easily go viral, leading to widespread panic and confusion. Misinformation can take many forms, from misleading news articles to manipulated images and videos, causing individuals to make ill-informed decisions based on unreliable sources. This can have serious consequences, such as inciting fear and division in communities, or even sparking public health crises. As technology continues to advance, it is crucial for society to be vigilant in verifying the accuracy of information and promoting critical thinking skills to combat the spread of misinformation and prevent unnecessary panic. By addressing this issue proactively, we can work towards creating a more informed and resilient society in the digital age.

LEVERAGING THE INTERNET FOR CRISIS MANAGEMENT

Given the increasing prevalence of crises in today's society, it is imperative to explore innovative strategies for efficient crisis management. One such approach is the utilization of the internet as a powerful tool for crisis response and communication. Leveraging the internet can enable real-time dissemination of information to a wide audience, facilitating rapid response and coordination among stakeholders. Moreover, social media platforms can be harnessed for crowd-sourced information gathering, enabling a more comprehensive understanding of the crisis and its implications. However, while the internet offers significant advantages in crisis management, it also presents challenges such as the spread of misinformation and the potential for information overload. Therefore, it is crucial for organizations to develop robust strategies for utilizing the internet effectively while mitigating its drawbacks. By harnessing the capabilities of the internet judiciously, organizations can enhance their crisis management efforts and improve overall resilience in the face of adversity.

XXXVI. INTERNET ADDICTION AND THE QUEST FOR INSTANT GRATIFICATION

The proliferation of the internet has brought about a new set of challenges, particularly in the realm of internet addiction. As individuals are constantly bombarded with information and stimuli, the quest for instant gratification has become a driving force behind excessive internet usage. This addiction to quick rewards and constant stimulation can have detrimental effects on individuals' mental health and overall well-being, leading to a range of negative consequences. Not only does internet addiction impair cognitive function and decision-making abilities, but it can also contribute to social isolation and deteriorating interpersonal relationships. Thus, it is essential to recognize the dangers of excessive internet use and work towards finding a balance that allows for the benefits of technology without succumbing to the pitfalls of instant gratification. By fostering awareness and implementing strategies to promote healthy internet habits, individuals can mitigate the negative impact of internet addiction on society.

THE NEED FOR IMMEDIATE RESPONSES

In the context of internet addiction and its impact on today's society, one of the critical aspects to consider is the need for immediate responses. As technology continues to advance at a rapid pace, individuals are becoming more reliant on digital devices and the internet for various aspects of their daily lives. This dependency can lead to addiction, which can have detrimental effects on individuals' mental, emotional, and physical well-being. Therefore, it is crucial for society to address this issue promptly and effectively. Immediate responses in the form of awareness campaigns, educational programs, and support systems can help individuals recognize and cope with internet addiction. By taking proactive measures to combat this growing problem, we can safeguard the mental health and overall quality of life of individuals in today's technology-driven world.

THE IMPACT ON PATIENCE AND PERSEVERANCE

In today's technologically-driven society, where instant gratification is a norm, the impact on patience and perseverance has become a significant concern. The ease of access to information, entertainment, and communication through the internet has led to a decrease in individuals' ability to wait for results or to stay committed to long-term goals. The constant need for stimulation and quick fixes has eroded the virtues of patience and perseverance, essential qualities for success in various aspects of life. As individuals become increasingly accustomed to instant responses and rewards, they may struggle to cope with challenges that require time and effort to overcome. This shift in mindset can have profound implications on personal development, relationships, and overall well-being. It is crucial for individuals to reevaluate their relationship with technology and cultivate patience and perseverance in order to thrive in a fast-paced digital world.

COUNTERACTING THE INSTANT GRATIFICATION CULTURE

Counteracting the instant gratification culture propagated by the digital age is essential in addressing the issue of internet addiction in today's society. One approach could be implementing educational programs that promote delayed gratification and self-control. Teaching individuals the benefits of patience and long-term rewards can help them resist the allure of instant gratification. Additionally, creating awareness campaigns that highlight the negative consequences of excessive screen time and internet use can also be effective in reducing addictive behaviors. Encouraging individuals to engage in offline activities that promote mindfulness, social interaction, and physical well-being can provide alternative sources of satisfaction that are not reliant on instant gratification. By promoting a culture of moderation, mindfulness, and balance, we can help individuals break free from the cycle of instant gratification and mitigate the harmful effects of internet addiction on society as a whole.

XXXVII. THE INFLUENCE OF INTERNET ADDICTION ON POLITICAL ENGAGEMENT

Internet addiction has become a prevalent issue in today's society, with individuals spending increasing amounts of time online. This addiction can have a significant impact on political engagement, as individuals may prioritize online activities over participation in civic and political life. The constant lure of social media, online gaming, and other internet activities can detract from important political discussions and actions. Research suggests that those who are addicted to the internet may be less likely to engage in political activities such as voting, attending rallies, and participating in advocacy efforts. This trend has led to concerns about the potential consequences for democratic participation and the overall health of political discourse. As such, it is crucial for policymakers and researchers to address the influence of internet addiction on political engagement in order to ensure a robust and participatory democracy.

ONLINE POLITICAL DISCOURSE

Online political discourse has become a crucial aspect of modern society, with the internet providing a platform for individuals to engage in political discussions, express their opinions, and mobilize for social change. However, while the internet has the potential to democratize political participation and provide a voice to marginalized groups, it also presents challenges such as the spread of misinformation, polarization, and echo chambers. As the digital landscape continues to evolve, it is essential for researchers to critically examine the impact of online political discourse on society. By understanding the dynamics of online political communication, we can develop strategies to promote informed and respectful discussions, counter misinformation, and bridge ideological divides. Ultimately, achieving a healthy and productive online political discourse is crucial for fostering a well-informed and engaged citizenry in today's digital age.

THE ROLE OF SOCIAL MEDIA IN ELECTIONS

Social media has become a ubiquitous tool in modern election campaigns, playing a significant role in shaping public opinion and political discourse. Platforms like Facebook, Twitter, and Instagram are now essential channels for candidates to reach voters and disseminate their messages. The ability to quickly share information and interact with a vast audience has revolutionized the way elections are conducted. However, the impact of social media on elections is not without controversy. The spread of misinformation, echo chambers, and targeted advertising have raised concerns about the manipulation of public opinion and democratic processes. Moreover, the prevalence of fake news and algorithmic bias can further polarize audiences and undermine the integrity of electoral outcomes. As we navigate the complex landscape of social media in elections, it is crucial to critically evaluate its role and potential consequences to ensure transparency, accountability, and fair democratic practices.

DIGITAL ACTIVISM AND CIVIC PARTICIPATION

Digital activism has emerged as a powerful tool for fostering civic engagement and participation in contemporary society. Through social media platforms, online campaigns, and other digital means, individuals are able to amplify their voices and mobilize support for various social and political causes. This has led to a democratization of activism, allowing for grassroots movements to gain momentum and challenge traditional power structures. However, the rise of digital activism also raises concerns about the potential for echo chambers and filter bubbles, where individuals are only exposed to like-minded perspectives, limiting critical thinking and dialogue. Furthermore, the rapid dissemination of information online can also lead to the spread of misinformation and fake news, which can undermine the credibility of digital activism efforts. As technology continues to play a central role in shaping societal discourse, it is essential to critically examine the double-edged sword of digital activism and its impact on civic participation.

XXXVIII. THE ROLE OF INTERNET ADDICTION IN CULTURAL PRESERVATION AND CHANGE

The role of internet addiction in cultural preservation and change is a complex and multifaceted issue that requires careful examination. On one hand, the internet has the potential to be a powerful tool for preserving and promoting cultural heritage, allowing for the dissemination of information and traditions to a global audience. However, excessive internet use can also lead to addiction, which may have a detrimental impact on individuals' engagement with their cultural practices and traditions. Internet addiction can result in a disconnect from one's cultural identity, as individuals become more absorbed in online activities and less involved in real-world cultural experiences. It is essential for researchers and policymakers to understand the ways in which internet addiction can affect cultural preservation and change, in order to develop strategies for promoting healthy internet usage while also safeguarding cultural heritage for future generations.

DIGITAL ARCHIVES AND CULTURAL HERITAGE

Digital archives play a crucial role in preserving and promoting cultural heritage in today's digital age. These online repositories hold vast amounts of cultural material, including documents, photographs, videos, and audio recordings, making them accessible to a global audience. By digitizing cultural artifacts, archives can protect them from physical deterioration and ensure their long-term preservation. Moreover, digital archives enable researchers, scholars, and the general public to easily access and engage with cultural heritage materials from anywhere in the world. However, the digitization of cultural heritage also raises concerns about issues such as data security, copyright infringement, and the potential loss of authenticity. Therefore, it is essential for institutions and individuals involved in creating digital archives to address these challenges through robust policies and practices to ensure the integrity and authenticity of cultural heritage materials online.

THE INTERNET'S IMPACT ON CULTURAL NORMS

The Internet has undeniably revolutionized the way in which we interact with one another and consume information, leading to significant shifts in cultural norms. The borderless nature of the Internet has facilitated an unprecedented exchange of ideas and traditions across different societies, resulting in the emergence of globalized cultural norms. This interconnectedness has led to the blurring of boundaries between cultures, as individuals can now easily access and adopt practices from around the world. However, this rapid dissemination of cultural norms also raises concerns about the potential erosion of traditional values and unique identities. Furthermore, the constant exposure to diverse cultural perspectives on the Internet may challenge established beliefs and norms within societies, leading to conflicts and tensions. Thus, while the Internet has undoubtedly broadened our cultural horizons, its impact on cultural norms is a double-edged sword that requires careful consideration and analysis.

THE BALANCE BETWEEN CULTURAL PRESERVATION AND INNOVATION

One of the key tensions in today's society lies in finding the balance between cultural preservation and innovation. On one hand, there is a growing emphasis on preserving traditional cultural practices, languages, and customs to safeguard heritage and identity. However, in the age of rapid technological advancement, there is also a push towards embracing innovation and new ways of thinking. This dilemma is particularly evident in the realm of internet addiction, where individuals are constantly bombarded with new technologies that can both enrich and detract from their cultural experiences. As our society grapples with the implications of internet addiction, it becomes crucial to strike a balance between preserving traditional values and embracing technological advancements. By navigating this delicate equilibrium, we can ensure that our cultural heritage remains intact while also harnessing the potential of innovation for the betterment of society.

XXXIX. INTERNET ADDICTION AND THE CHANGING LANDSCAPE OF MEDIA CONSUMPTION

As technology continues to advance at a rapid pace, the ways in which individuals consume media are constantly evolving. With the rise of the internet, a new form of addiction has emerged that has garnered increasing attention from researchers and policymakers: internet addiction. This addictive behavior associated with excessive internet use has profound implications for society as a whole. It not only affects individuals' mental and physical health but also transforms the landscape of media consumption. As people spend more time online, traditional forms of media such as television and print media are being overshadowed by digital platforms. This shift not only alters the way information is disseminated but also impacts the advertising industry and societal norms. Understanding the complex relationship between internet addiction and changing media consumption patterns is crucial for addressing the challenges posed by excessive internet use in today's digital age.

SHIFT FROM TRADITIONAL TO DIGITAL MEDIA

The shift from traditional to digital media has revolutionized the way information is disseminated and consumed in modern society. This transition has seen a significant increase in the use of online platforms for news, entertainment, and communication, leading to a democratization of information where individuals can access a vast array of content at their fingertips. However, as technology continues to advance, concerns have emerged regarding the potential negative impacts of excessive screen time and internet addiction on individuals' mental health and social relationships. It is imperative for researchers and policymakers to address these issues and develop strategies to promote a healthy balance between online and offline activities to mitigate the adverse effects of technology on today's society. The evolution of media from print to digital offers unparalleled opportunities for connectivity and knowledge-sharing, but it is essential to navigate this landscape with caution to safeguard our well-being.

BINGE-WATCHING AND STREAMING SERVICES

Binge-watching and streaming services have become prevalent in today's society, offering viewers the convenience of watching multiple episodes or movies consecutively. While this trend has revolutionized the way we consume entertainment, it also poses potential risks in terms of internet addiction. With the accessibility and endless options available on platforms like Netflix and Hulu, individuals may find themselves spending excessive amounts of time online, leading to negative consequences on their physical and mental health. Studies have shown that prolonged screen time can lead to sleep disturbances, eye strain, and decreased social interactions. Therefore, it is crucial for researchers and policymakers to address the impact of binge-watching on society and develop strategies to promote a healthy balance between technology use and overall well-being. By understanding the double sides of technology, we can navigate the digital landscape more mindfully and responsibly.

THE FUTURE OF MEDIA AND ENTERTAINMENT

The future of media and entertainment is taking a transformative turn with the rapid advancement of technology. With the rise of virtual and augmented reality, artificial intelligence, and immersive experiences, the way we consume media and entertainment is evolving at a rapid pace. These technologies are reshaping the way content is created, distributed, and experienced by audiences. The convergence of traditional forms of media with cutting-edge technology is creating new opportunities for storytelling, engagement, and interactivity. As we move forward, it is essential for researchers and industry professionals to explore the implications of these advancements on society, culture, and individual behavior. Understanding how these developments impact issues like internet addiction, mental health, and social relationships will be crucial in shaping a responsible and sustainable future for media and entertainment. By staying ahead of the curve and critically analyzing the double-sided nature of technology, we can navigate the challenges and opportunities that lie ahead in this dynamic field.

XL. THE ROLE OF INTERNET ADDICTION IN PERSONAL FINANCE MANAGEMENT

The increasing prevalence of internet addiction has significant implications for personal finance management. Individuals who are addicted to the internet may engage in excessive online shopping, impulse buying, or risky financial behaviors, leading to detrimental effects on their financial well-being. This dependence on the internet for shopping and entertainment can result in overspending, debt accumulation, and ultimately hinder one's ability to save or invest wisely. Moreover, the constant access to online platforms may create a false sense of security and instant gratification, making it challenging for individuals to set and adhere to financial goals. As a result, it is crucial for individuals to recognize the impact of internet addiction on their financial habits and seek strategies to mitigate its negative effects, such as implementing budgeting tools, practicing mindfulness in spending, and seeking support from financial advisors or counselors. By addressing the role of internet addiction in personal finance management, individuals can take steps towards financial stability and well-being.

ONLINE BANKING AND FINANCIAL PLANNING

Online banking and financial planning have become integral aspects of modern society, simplifying the way individuals manage their finances. The convenience of online banking allows customers to access their accounts, transfer funds, and pay bills from the comfort of their own homes. Moreover, online financial planning tools offer personalized budgeting and savings strategies, helping individuals achieve their financial goals efficiently. However, the rise of online banking has also exposed individuals to cyber threats and security breaches, raising concerns about the safety of personal and financial information. As technology continues to advance, it is crucial for individuals to be mindful of the potential risks associated with online banking and take proactive measures to safeguard their financial data. By striking a balance between convenience and security, individuals can fully leverage the benefits of online banking while protecting their financial well-being.

THE RISE OF FINTECH AND INVESTMENT APPS

The rise of fintech and investment apps has revolutionized the way individuals engage with financial markets, offering increased accessibility and convenience for users. These technological advancements have democratized investing by allowing individuals to easily access and manage their portfolios from the comfort of their own homes. With the proliferation of these apps, individuals can now make informed investment decisions based on real-time data and analysis, without the need for expensive financial advisors or traditional brokerage services. However, this increased ease of access also presents potential risks, as inexperienced users may be more susceptible to making impulsive investment decisions or falling victim to scams. As fintech continues to reshape the financial landscape, it is essential for users to educate themselves on best practices and risk management strategies to ensure they make sound investment choices in an increasingly digital world.

THE RISK OF ONLINE GAMBLING AND FINANCIAL SCAMS

The risk of online gambling and financial scams is a pressing concern in today's society, particularly with the increasing accessibility and popularity of online platforms. The anonymity and convenience offered by the internet make it easier for individuals to engage in risky behaviors without fully understanding the potential consequences. Online gambling, in particular, has been linked to addictive behaviors and financial ruin for many individuals who fall victim to its allure. Similarly, financial scams have become more sophisticated and widespread, targeting vulnerable populations who may not have the knowledge or resources to protect themselves. These risks highlight the need for increased education and regulation to protect consumers from the pitfalls of online activities. By addressing these issues through comprehensive strategies that emphasize consumer protection and financial literacy, we can work towards a safer and more secure digital landscape for all individuals.

XLI. THE IMPACT OF INTERNET ADDICTION ON TRAVEL AND EXPLORATION

The impact of internet addiction on travel and exploration can be significant in today's society. As individuals become more engrossed in their online activities, they may spend less time engaging in real-world experiences such as travel and exploration. Internet addiction can lead to a sedentary lifestyle, where individuals prefer to stay indoors and engage with their devices rather than venture out into the world. This can have negative implications for personal growth, mental well-being, and cultural understanding. Additionally, excessive internet use can diminish the desire for real-life experiences, leading to a decrease in tourism and exploration. As technology continues to advance, it is crucial to understand the repercussions of internet addiction on travel and exploration and to find ways to balance the benefits of technology with the need for real-world experiences.

VIRTUAL TOURISM AND DIGITAL EXPLORATION

Virtual tourism and digital exploration have revolutionized the way individuals experience travel and adventure. Through virtual reality technologies and online platforms, people can immerse themselves in faraway destinations without leaving the comfort of their homes. This has opened up a new realm of possibilities for those who may not have the means or opportunity to travel physically. However, while virtual tourism offers unprecedented access to different parts of the world, it also raises questions about the authenticity of these experiences and the impact on local communities. As scholars delve deeper into the implications of this digital shift in tourism, it becomes crucial to assess the balance between the benefits of virtual exploration and the potential drawbacks, such as cultural commodification and environmental repercussions. Understanding the complexities of virtual tourism is vital for shaping responsible and sustainable practices in the digital age.

THE INFLUENCE OF SOCIAL MEDIA ON TRAVEL CHOICES

The influence of social media on travel choices has become increasingly significant in today's society. With the rise of platforms such as Instagram, Facebook, and Pinterest, individuals are constantly bombarded with images and reviews of various destinations, influencing their decision-making process when it comes to travel. Social media not only serves as a source of inspiration but also as a medium for sharing tips, recommendations, and experiences with like-minded individuals. Through social media, travelers can access real-time information about different locations, accommodations, and activities, allowing them to make more informed choices. However, the overwhelming amount of information available on these platforms can also lead to decision paralysis and unrealistic expectations. It is crucial for travelers to critically evaluate the information they encounter on social media and make decisions that align with their own preferences and values to ensure a fulfilling travel experience.

THE BENEFITS AND DRAWBACKS OF ONLINE TRAVEL PLANNING

Online travel planning offers numerous benefits, including convenience, cost savings, and a vast array of options for accommodations, activities, and transportation. Travelers can research destinations, read reviews, and compare prices with just a few clicks, saving time and effort. Additionally, online booking platforms often offer exclusive deals and discounts, making it more affordable for individuals to plan their trips. However, there are also drawbacks to online travel planning that must be considered. The abundance of choices can be overwhelming, leading to decision fatigue and information overload. Furthermore, relying solely on online resources may result in missing out on personalized recommendations and local insights that can enhance the overall travel experience. Therefore, while online travel planning offers many advantages, it is essential for travelers to strike a balance between digital convenience and authentic travel experiences.

XLII. INTERNET ADDICTION AND THE EVOLUTION OF RETAIL

The evolution of retail in the age of internet addiction presents a complex and multifaceted challenge for businesses and consumers alike. As individuals become increasingly reliant on the convenience and accessibility of online shopping, the traditional brick-and-mortar retail experience is forced to adapt in order to remain relevant and competitive. The shift towards e-commerce has fundamentally altered the way in which goods and services are bought and sold, leading to a redefinition of consumer behavior and expectations. While the internet offers unparalleled convenience and choice, it also facilitates compulsive and addictive behaviors that can have detrimental effects on mental health and financial well-being. As retailers navigate this changing landscape, it is crucial to address the impact of internet addiction on consumer habits and preferences. By understanding the interplay between technology and consumer behavior, businesses can develop strategies to better serve their customers while promoting healthy shopping practices.

THE GROWTH OF E-COMMERCE

E-commerce has experienced exponential growth in recent years, revolutionizing the way businesses operate and how consumers engage in shopping activities. This surge in online retailing can be attributed to advancements in technology, increased internet penetration, and shifting consumer preferences towards convenience and accessibility. The convenience of being able to shop from the comfort of one's own home, coupled with the ability to compare prices and products within seconds, has propelled e-commerce to the forefront of retailing. Moreover, the rise of mobile e-commerce has further accelerated this growth, as smartphone usage continues to soar globally. As e-commerce continues to evolve and expand, it is crucial for businesses to adapt to these changes and harness the power of online platforms to stay competitive in today's digital landscape. Additionally, policymakers must address the regulatory challenges associated with e-commerce to ensure a fair and transparent marketplace for all parties involved.

THE DECLINE OF BRICK-AND-MORTAR STORES

One of the most significant impacts of technology on today's society is the decline of brick-and-mortar stores. With the rise of e-commerce giants like Amazon, traditional retail stores are struggling to compete in the digital age. Convenience, lower prices, and a wider selection of products online have led many consumers to shift their shopping habits away from physical stores. This trend has been exacerbated by the COVID-19 pandemic, which forced many brick-and-mortar stores to temporarily close their doors, causing a further decline in foot traffic. As a result, many retail chains have been forced to downsize or declare bankruptcy, leading to job losses and economic instability in many communities. The challenge for brick-and-mortar stores moving forward will be to adapt to the changing retail landscape and find ways to differentiate themselves from their online competitors in order to survive in this increasingly digital world.

THE FUTURE OF RETAIL IN A DIGITAL WORLD

The future of retail in a digital world is rapidly evolving, driven by technological advancements and changing consumer behaviors. As e-commerce continues to expand, traditional brick-and-mortar stores are faced with the challenge of adapting to stay relevant in the competitive market. The integration of online and offline shopping experiences through omnichannel strategies has become essential for retailers to provide a seamless and personalized customer journey. With the rise of artificial intelligence and big data analytics, retailers can gain valuable insights into consumer preferences and behavior, enabling them to tailor their offerings and marketing strategies accordingly. Moreover, the use of virtual and augmented reality technologies has the potential to revolutionize the way consumers shop by providing immersive and interactive experiences. However, as retailers embrace digital innovations, they must also address concerns surrounding data privacy and security to build and maintain consumer trust in the digital landscape. The future of retail in a digital world holds immense possibilities for enhancing the shopping experience, but it also presents challenges that require strategic planning and adaptation.

THE POTENTIAL FOR DISTRACTION AND PROCRASTINATION

The potential for distraction and procrastination in today's society has exponentially increased with the widespread use of technology, particularly the internet. The limitless access to social media, online games, and streaming platforms provides constant stimuli that can easily divert individuals from their tasks at hand. This phenomenon can lead to decreased productivity, poor time management, and ultimately, a sense of dissatisfaction with one's accomplishments. Moreover, the instant gratification and entertainment offered by digital distractions can fuel procrastination tendencies, making it difficult for individuals to focus on important tasks and meet deadlines. As a result, it is crucial for individuals to develop self-discipline and establish boundaries in their technology usage to mitigate the adverse effects of distraction and procrastination on their daily lives. By understanding these challenges, we can work towards finding effective strategies to harness the benefits of technology while minimizing its drawbacks.

BALANCING ONLINE RESOURCES WITH PERSONAL DEVELOPMENT GOALS

In today's digital age, striking a balance between utilizing online resources for personal development goals while avoiding the pitfalls of internet addiction is a paramount concern. It is crucial for individuals to harness the vast array of information and educational opportunities available online to enhance their skills, knowledge, and personal growth. However, excessive reliance on digital platforms can lead to negative consequences such as decreased productivity, social isolation, and mental health issues. Thus, individuals must actively manage their online consumption, setting limits, and boundaries to ensure that online activities are aligned with their personal development objectives. By being mindful of their online behaviors and consciously choosing how to engage with technology, individuals can maximize the benefits of online resources while safeguarding their mental well-being and overall personal growth. Finding the equilibrium between online resources and personal development goals is essential in navigating the complexities of the digital world to thrive in today's society.

XLIV. INTERNET ADDICTION AND THE CONCEPT OF PRIVACY

Internet addiction has become a pressing issue in today's society, with individuals spending excessive amounts of time online to the detriment of their physical and mental well-being. One key aspect that exacerbates this addiction is the erosion of privacy in the digital age. As more and more personal information is shared online, individuals are constantly exposed to targeted advertisements, data breaches, and potential privacy violations. The concept of privacy, once a fundamental right, is now blurred in the realm of the internet, where algorithms track and analyze users' every move. This loss of privacy not only contributes to the addictive nature of the internet but also raises ethical concerns about the manipulation and exploitation of individuals for profit. As we grapple with the consequences of internet addiction, it is crucial to also consider the implications on privacy and the need for robust regulatory measures to protect individuals in the digital age.

SHARING PERSONAL INFORMATION ONLINE

Sharing personal information online has become a common practice in today's digital age. While the Internet provides a platform for connecting with others and sharing aspects of one's life, it also opens individuals up to potential privacy risks and security concerns. As more people participate in social media and online communities, the amount of personal information being shared continues to grow exponentially. This proliferation of personal data can lead to issues such as identity theft, online harassment, and cyberbullying. It is essential for individuals to carefully consider the potential consequences of sharing personal information online and to take steps to protect their privacy and security. By being mindful of the information they share and implementing robust privacy settings, individuals can mitigate the risks associated with sharing personal information online and safeguard their digital identities.

THE EROSION OF PRIVACY IN THE DIGITAL AGE

A critical issue facing society in the digital age is the erosion of privacy. With the proliferation of online platforms, social media, and data collection practices, individuals are increasingly vulnerable to having their personal information exposed or exploited without their consent. This erosion of privacy poses significant ethical and societal concerns, as it raises questions about the balance between technological advancements and individual rights. As digital technologies continue to evolve, there is a growing need for safeguards and regulations to protect people's privacy in the online realm. Without adequate measures in place, there is a risk of further encroachment on individuals' privacy, leading to potential implications for autonomy, freedom, and democracy. It is imperative for policymakers, technology companies, and individuals alike to address these challenges and strive towards creating a digital landscape that respects and upholds the right to privacy.

STRATEGIES FOR PROTECTING PERSONAL PRIVACY ONLINE

In today's digital age, personal privacy online is a frequently discussed and hotly debated topic. As technology continues to advance exponentially, individuals must be vigilant in protecting their personal information from falling into the wrong hands. There are several strategies that can be implemented to safeguard personal privacy online, including using strong and unique passwords for each online account, enabling two-factor authentication whenever possible, regularly updating privacy settings on social media platforms, being cautious when sharing personal information on websites, and using reputable virtual private networks (VPNs) to encrypt internet connections. By employing these strategies, individuals can mitigate the risks of personal information being compromised and maintain a sense of control over their online privacy. In an era where data breaches and cyberattacks are increasingly common, taking proactive measures to protect personal privacy online is essential for preserving digital security and trust in the online landscape.

XLV. THE ROLE OF INTERNET ADDICTION IN SHAPING IDENTITY

In examining the role of internet addiction in shaping identity, it is imperative to consider the profound influence that excessive online engagement can have on individuals' sense of self. The internet provides a platform for individuals to explore different personas, connect with like-minded individuals, and seek validation and acceptance. However, when internet use becomes compulsive and interferes with daily functioning, it can lead to a distortion of one's self-perception and identity formation. The allure of online worlds and the instant gratification they provide can lead individuals to prioritize their online personas over their real-life interactions and responsibilities. This shift in focus can result in a loss of authentic self-expression and a reliance on external validation for a sense of self-worth. Ultimately, internet addiction has the potential to mold individuals' identities in ways that prioritize virtual connections over real-world experiences, leading to a disconnect between one's online and offline selves.

ONLINE PERSONAS AND REAL-LIFE IMPLICATIONS

The phenomenon of online personas and its real-life implications have become increasingly pertinent in today's digital age. As individuals engage in creating and curating their online identities through social media platforms, they often project idealized versions of themselves to the world. These personas may not always align perfectly with their true selves, leading to a disconnect between online and offline personalities. This discrepancy can have profound implications for mental health, self-esteem, and personal relationships. Studies have shown that excessive reliance on online personas can contribute to feelings of loneliness, depression, and anxiety. Furthermore, the pressure to maintain a certain image online can lead to a lack of authenticity and authenticity in real-life interactions. It is essential for individuals to be mindful of the impact of their online personas on their overall well-being and actively strive for greater congruence between their digital and physical selves.

THE SEARCH FOR IDENTITY IN THE DIGITAL REALM

In the digital realm, where individuals can curate and construct online personas, the search for identity takes on a multifaceted and complex nature. As people navigate social media platforms, online forums, and virtual communities, they are constantly faced with the challenge of defining themselves in this evolving landscape. The allure of anonymity and the ability to present a curated version of oneself can lead to a sense of freedom and self-expression, but it also raises questions about authenticity and the true self. The quest for identity in the digital realm is intertwined with issues of self-presentation, validation, and the impact of external validation on one's sense of self-worth. As technology continues to shape our interactions and perceptions of ourselves, it is crucial to critically examine the implications of these digital identities on individuals and society as a whole.

THE INFLUENCE OF ONLINE COMMUNITIES ON SELF-PERCEPTION

The influence of online communities on self-perception is a complex and multifaceted topic that requires careful examination. Online communities have the potential to both positively and negatively impact individuals' self-perception. On one hand, these communities can provide a sense of belonging, support, and validation, which can enhance individuals' self-esteem and self-worth. However, on the other hand, online communities can also perpetuate unrealistic beauty standards, lead to comparison, and contribute to feelings of inadequacy and low self-esteem. It is essential to consider the ways in which individuals interact with online communities and how these interactions shape their perception of themselves. Understanding the nuances of this relationship is crucial for addressing the potential harms of online communities and promoting positive self-perception in today's society.

XLVI. INTERNET ADDICTION AND THE NOTION OF TIME MANAGEMENT

The concept of internet addiction is a growing concern in today's society, with individuals becoming increasingly reliant on their digital devices for entertainment, communication, and work. One of the key issues associated with internet addiction is the impact it has on time management. As individuals spend more time online, they often neglect other important tasks and responsibilities in their lives, leading to a sense of imbalance and loss of control. This lack of time management can have serious consequences on one's mental health, productivity, and overall well-being. It is crucial for individuals to recognize the signs of internet addiction and take proactive steps to manage their time effectively. By setting boundaries, establishing priorities, and seeking support when needed, individuals can regain control over their time and reduce the negative effects of internet addiction on their daily lives.

THE PERCEPTION OF TIME SPENT ONLINE

The perception of time spent online is a critical aspect of understanding internet addiction and its impact on today's society. Individuals vary in how they perceive the time they spend online; some may feel a sense of accomplishment and productivity, while others may experience guilt or anxiety over excessive screen time. This perception is influenced by factors such as social norms, personal beliefs, and cultural influences. Research has shown that excessive internet use can lead to negative consequences, including impaired social functioning, decreased cognitive abilities, and even physical health issues. It is important for researchers and practitioners to consider how individuals perceive their online behavior in order to develop effective interventions and strategies for mitigating the harmful effects of internet addiction. By understanding the perception of time spent online, we can better address the complexities of technology use in today's society.

TOOLS AND TECHNIQUES FOR EFFECTIVE TIME MANAGEMENT

Tools and techniques for effective time management are crucial in today's fast-paced society, particularly as the reliance on technology continues to grow. One method that has been proven effective is the use of time tracking apps, which can help individuals monitor their activities and identify time-wasting habits. Another useful tool is the Eisenhower Matrix, which categorizes tasks based on their urgency and importance, allowing for better prioritization. Additionally, the Pomodoro Technique, using intervals of focused work followed by short breaks, has been shown to enhance productivity and prevent burnout. By utilizing these tools in conjunction with setting clear goals, establishing routines, and practicing self-discipline, individuals can effectively manage their time in an increasingly digital world. These strategies not only promote efficiency and effectiveness but also help combat the negative impacts of technology-induced distractions on daily life.

THE CHALLENGE OF BALANCING ONLINE AND OFFLINE TIME

The challenge of balancing online and offline time in today's society has become increasingly complex with the widespread availability and accessibility of technology. As individuals are constantly surrounded by smartphones, computers, and other devices, finding a healthy equilibrium between digital and real-world interactions has become a pressing issue. This balancing act is crucial for maintaining mental well-being, social relationships, and overall productivity. Excessive time spent online can lead to feelings of isolation, anxiety, and a decreased sense of presence in the physical world. On the other hand, completely disconnecting from the online world may result in missed opportunities for learning, communication, and connection. Therefore, individuals must strive to find a middle ground that allows for the benefits of technology while also prioritizing meaningful face-to-face interactions and self-care activities. By actively managing one's online and offline activities, individuals can mitigate the negative impacts of excessive screen time and ensure a more balanced and fulfilling lifestyle.

XLVII. THE ROLE OF INTERNET ADDICTION IN LIFESTYLE CHOICES

Internet addiction has emerged as a significant concern in modern society, impacting various aspects of individuals' lifestyle choices. The excessive use of the internet can lead to detrimental effects on physical health, social relationships, and overall well-being. Research indicates that individuals who are addicted to the internet often prioritize online activities over real-life interactions, leading to a decline in face-to-face communication and social skills. Moreover, the constant connectivity and instant gratification provided by the internet can contribute to unhealthy habits such as sleep deprivation, poor dietary choices, and sedentary behavior. As such, understanding the role of internet addiction in lifestyle choices is crucial for addressing the negative consequences associated with excessive internet use and promoting a balanced approach to technology in today's society.

THE INFLUENCE ON HEALTH AND FITNESS ROUTINES

In today's society, the influence of technology on health and fitness routines cannot be understated. While technological advancements have led to the proliferation of fitness apps, wearable devices, and online resources that can aid individuals in achieving their health goals, there is also a growing concern about the negative impact of excessive screen time and sedentary behavior on overall well-being. The convenience of virtual workouts and remote monitoring can promote a more active lifestyle, but it can also contribute to a sedentary lifestyle if not balanced with physical activity. Moreover, the addictive nature of technology, particularly social media and gaming, can lead to internet addiction, which further hinders individuals from engaging in healthy habits. As researchers continue to explore the double-edged sword of technology on health and fitness, it is crucial for individuals to find a balance that maximizes the benefits while minimizing the risks associated with excessive screen time and sedentary behavior.

DIGITAL DETOX AND WELLNESS TRENDS

The increasing prevalence of digital detox and wellness trends in today's society highlights a growing awareness of the potential negative impact of technology on mental and physical well-being. As individuals experience heightened levels of stress, anxiety, and burnout from constant connectivity, the concept of unplugging and taking breaks from screens has gained traction as a way to rejuvenate and recenter. Digital detox retreats, mindfulness apps, and wellness practices are emerging as popular solutions to combat the adverse effects of internet addiction. However, while these trends offer a promising avenue for promoting self-care and balance in a technology-driven world, it is crucial to critically evaluate their efficacy and sustainability in addressing the root causes of excessive screen time. As researchers delve deeper into understanding the nuances of digital detox and wellness interventions, it becomes imperative to explore their long-term implications for individual well-being and societal norms.

THE INTEGRATION OF TECHNOLOGY IN DAILY LIFE

The integration of technology in daily life has become pervasive, revolutionizing how individuals communicate, work, and interact with the world around them. With the rise of smartphones, tablets, and other digital devices, people are constantly connected to a vast network of information and social relationships. This seamless connectivity has transformed the way we access information, conduct business, and entertain ourselves. However, this reliance on technology has also raised concerns about internet addiction and its impact on society. While technology offers numerous benefits, such as increased efficiency and convenience, excessive use can lead to negative consequences, such as isolation, sleep disturbances, and decreased productivity. It is crucial for individuals to strike a balance between utilizing technology effectively and maintaining healthy boundaries to prevent the onset of internet addiction and its detrimental effects on mental health and overall well-being.

XLVIII. INTERNET ADDICTION AND THE CONCEPT OF REALITY

The prevalence of internet addiction has raised concerns about its impact on individuals' perception of reality. As individuals spend more time online, they may become disconnected from the tangible world around them, blurring the lines between virtual and physical realities. This can lead to a distorted sense of self, as individuals may prioritize their online personas over their real-life relationships and responsibilities. Additionally, the constant exposure to curated content on social media platforms further exacerbates this issue, creating unrealistic standards and expectations for individuals. It is crucial to recognize the potential consequences of internet addiction on one's perception of reality and take steps to address this issue. By promoting digital literacy and mindfulness, individuals can develop a healthier relationship with technology and maintain a balanced perspective on the virtual world and the tangible reality.

VIRTUAL REALITY AND AUGMENTED REALITY EXPERIENCES

Virtual Reality (VR) and Augmented Reality (AR) experiences have become prominent features in today's society, offering innovative ways to interact with digital content. These technologies provide users with immersive, realistic experiences that can enhance learning, training, entertainment, and even therapeutic interventions. The use of VR and AR has the potential to revolutionize various industries, including healthcare, education, gaming, and marketing. By allowing users to engage with digital environments in a more interactive and engaging manner, VR and AR experiences can significantly impact the way individuals perceive and interact with the world around them. However, as these technologies become more prevalent, concerns about privacy, ethical implications, and potential addiction have also surfaced. It is essential for researchers and practitioners to carefully examine the double-sided nature of VR and AR experiences to maximize their benefits while minimizing their drawbacks in today's society.

THE BLURRING OF LINES BETWEEN VIRTUAL AND ACTUAL REALITIES

In contemporary society, the boundaries between virtual and actual realities are becoming increasingly blurred, raising significant concerns about the impact of this phenomenon on individuals and society as a whole. With the widespread use of immersive technologies such as virtual reality, augmented reality, and social media platforms, individuals are spending more time in digital environments, often at the expense of real-world interactions and experiences. This shift raises questions about the potential consequences of such behavior on mental health, social relationships, and overall well-being. Additionally, the constant connectivity afforded by these technologies has led to a sense of detachment and disconnection from the physical world, further complicating the distinction between virtual and actual realities. As researchers delve deeper into understanding the implications of this blurring of lines, it becomes increasingly critical to address the ethical, psychological, and societal implications of our evolving relationship with technology.

THE PSYCHOLOGICAL EFFECTS OF IMMERSIVE TECHNOLOGIES

The psychological effects of immersive technologies have become a pressing concern in today's society, as individuals increasingly find themselves engrossed in virtual worlds and disconnected from reality. Research has shown that prolonged use of immersive technologies such as virtual reality or augmented reality can lead to symptoms resembling addiction, including withdrawal, tolerance, and cravings. These technologies have the potential to alter individuals' perception of self and reality, blurring the boundaries between the virtual and physical worlds. This can result in a disconnect from real-world relationships and responsibilities, leading to increased feelings of loneliness, anxiety, and depression. As immersive technologies continue to advance and become more accessible, it is crucial for researchers and policymakers to address the potential psychological impact on individuals and society as a whole. By understanding and mitigating these effects, we can harness the benefits of immersive technologies while minimizing their negative consequences.

XLIX. THE ROLE OF INTERNET ADDICTION IN COMMUNITY BUILDING

The role of internet addiction in community building, as explored in this doctoral research, presents a complex interplay between technology and social dynamics. Internet addiction, characterized by excessive use of online platforms to the detriment of one's daily functioning, can have significant implications for community cohesion and interaction. On one hand, the internet offers unprecedented opportunities for individuals to connect, collaborate, and engage with a global audience, thereby fostering community building on a scale never before possible. However, excessive internet use leading to addiction may also isolate individuals from physical community interactions and diminish the quality of face-to-face relationships. Understanding the impact of internet addiction on community building is crucial in developing strategies to mitigate its negative consequences while harnessing the potential of online connectivity for enhancing social cohesion in today's society.

ONLINE COMMUNITIES AND SOCIAL SUPPORT

Online communities have become a prevalent source of social support for individuals in today's society, offering a platform for connection and interaction with like-minded individuals. These virtual spaces provide opportunities for individuals to share experiences, seek advice, and receive emotional support from others facing similar challenges. Research has shown that online communities can have a significant impact on well-being, offering a sense of belonging and reducing feelings of isolation. However, it is essential to acknowledge the potential drawbacks of reliance on online communities for social support, such as the development of internet addiction and a decrease in face-to-face social interactions. Understanding the double-sided nature of online communities and considering the implications of excessive use is crucial in promoting a balanced approach to utilizing technology for social support.

THE POTENTIAL FOR ECHO CHAMBERS AND POLARIZATION

The proliferation of digital technologies has revolutionized the way information is shared and consumed, leading to the rise of echo chambers and polarization in online spaces. Echo chambers are virtual spaces where individuals are exposed only to information that aligns with their existing beliefs, reinforcing their worldview and creating a feedback loop of confirmation bias. This phenomenon can result in a narrowing of perspectives, a diminished capacity for critical thinking, and an exacerbation of polarization within society. As individuals retreat into these digital enclaves, they are less likely to engage with diverse viewpoints, leading to a fragmentation of public discourse and an erosion of empathy. In order to address the negative consequences of echo chambers and polarization, it is crucial for individuals to actively seek out diverse perspectives, engage in civil discourse, and critically evaluate the information they encounter online. Only by promoting dialogue and understanding can we mitigate the harmful effects of echo chambers and polarization in the digital age.

FOSTERING INCLUSIVE AND DIVERSE ONLINE SPACES

Fostering inclusive and diverse online spaces is crucial in addressing the issue of internet addiction and its impact on today's society. By creating environments that welcome individuals from all backgrounds, cultures, and identities, online spaces can provide a sense of belonging and connection that may help mitigate the potential isolation and disconnection that can lead to excessive internet use. Strategies such as implementing diverse representation in media, promoting respectful communication, and actively combating discrimination and harassment online are key to fostering inclusivity. Additionally, creating opportunities for individuals to engage with different perspectives and learn from each other can help promote understanding and empathy, thus reducing the likelihood of using the internet as a means of escapism or avoidance. Ultimately, by prioritizing inclusivity and diversity in online spaces, we can work towards a healthier and more balanced relationship with technology in today's society.

L. INTERNET ADDICTION AND THE PURSUIT OF HAPPINESS

Internet addiction is a growing concern in today's society, with individuals spending increasing amounts of time online, often at the expense of real-world relationships and responsibilities. The pursuit of happiness, a fundamental human desire, can be hindered by an addiction to the virtual world, as it can lead to feelings of isolation, anxiety, and depression. Studies have shown that excessive internet use can disrupt the brain's reward system, similar to the effects of substance abuse, making it difficult for individuals to feel satisfied with offline experiences. Moreover, the constant stimulation and instant gratification offered by the internet can create a cycle of compulsive behavior that is hard to break. As researchers delve deeper into the impact of internet addiction on mental health and well-being, it becomes increasingly clear that finding a balance between online and offline activities is essential for a fulfilling and happy life.

THE SEARCH FOR FULFILLMENT ONLINE

In the realm of online interactions, the search for fulfillment is a prevalent and complex phenomenon. Individuals turn to the internet seeking connection, validation, and purpose. Whether through social media platforms, online communities, or digital therapy services, the virtual world offers a plethora of avenues for individuals to explore and navigate in their quest for fulfillment. This search is fueled by the inherent human need for belonging and self-actualization, which are often amplified by the affordances of the digital landscape. However, the allure of instant gratification and the omnipresence of technology can also lead to detrimental consequences, such as internet addiction and social isolation. As technology continues to reshape the ways in which individuals seek fulfillment online, it is crucial to analyze the double-edged sword that is the digital age, understanding both its benefits and drawbacks on today's society.

THE ROLE OF DOPAMINE IN ONLINE ACTIVITIES

Dopamine, a neurotransmitter associated with pleasure and reward, plays a crucial role in online activities and internet addiction. When individuals engage in online activities such as social media, gaming, or online shopping, dopamine is released in the brain, creating a sense of satisfaction and pleasure. This can lead to compulsive behavior and a reinforcement loop where individuals seek more online engagement to experience the same level of satisfaction. However, excessive dopamine release from prolonged online activities can dysregulate the brain's reward system, leading to addiction and dependency. Understanding the role of dopamine in online activities is essential in addressing the growing concern of internet addiction and its impact on society. By elucidating the mechanisms behind dopamine's involvement in online behaviors, interventions and strategies can be developed to prevent and treat internet addiction effectively.

THE QUEST FOR A BALANCED AND HAPPY LIFE

The quest for a balanced and happy life is a fundamental aspect of human existence and is closely intertwined with the impact of technology on today's society. In a digital era where individuals are constantly connected, the pursuit of balance between online and offline activities becomes increasingly challenging. While technology offers immense benefits in terms of communication, information access, and convenience, it also poses significant risks, such as internet addiction. This addiction can disrupt personal relationships, lead to health issues, and contribute to a decline in overall well-being. Therefore, it is imperative for individuals to develop strategies to maintain a healthy balance in their use of technology, prioritizing real-world connections, physical activity, and self-care practices. By consciously managing their digital consumption, individuals can strive towards a more harmonious and fulfilling life, free from the negative impacts of excessive technology use.

LI. THE ROLE OF INTERNET ADDICTION IN ENVIRONMENTAL ACTIVISM

Internet addiction plays a significant role in shaping environmental activism in today's society. As individuals spend more time online, they are increasingly exposed to information and campaigns related to environmental issues. This heightened awareness can lead to increased engagement in activism, as people become more connected with like-minded individuals and organizations through online platforms. However, the downside of internet addiction in this context is the potential for individuals to become so engulfed in their online activities that they neglect real-world action and tangible solutions to environmental problems. This over-reliance on technology can create a disconnect between individuals and the natural world, hindering the effectiveness of environmental activism efforts. Therefore, it is crucial to strike a balance between utilizing the internet as a tool for raising awareness and mobilizing support, while also taking concrete actions in the physical world to address environmental challenges.

ONLINE PLATFORMS FOR ENVIRONMENTAL ADVOCACY

Online platforms have become powerful tools for environmental advocacy, allowing individuals and organizations to reach a global audience and raise awareness about pressing environmental issues. Social media platforms, in particular, have enabled users to share information, organize events, and mobilize support for environmental causes. By leveraging the viral nature of online content, environmental advocates can amplify their message and spark meaningful conversations about sustainability and conservation. Online platforms also facilitate collaboration among like-minded individuals and facilitate the exchange of ideas and best practices in environmental advocacy. However, the effectiveness of online platforms for environmental advocacy can be hindered by the spread of misinformation and the polarization of discussions. As such, it is crucial for environmental advocates to critically evaluate the information they share online and strive to promote accurate and balanced narratives to ensure the credibility of the environmental movement in the digital age.

THE SPREAD OF ENVIRONMENTAL AWARENESS

The spread of environmental awareness has been a key focus in recent years as society grapples with the effects of climate change and other environmental challenges. In today's interconnected world, the internet has played a crucial role in promoting environmental awareness on a global scale. Social media platforms and online campaigns have allowed individuals to easily share information, mobilize support for environmental causes, and hold corporations and governments accountable for their impact on the environment. However, the same technology that enables the spread of environmental awareness also poses challenges, such as the rise of internet addiction and its potential negative impact on individuals' engagement with environmental issues. As we navigate the double-edged sword of technology's impact on society, it is essential for researchers and policymakers to consider how to harness the power of the internet for positive change while mitigating its potential drawbacks.

DIGITAL CAMPAIGNS AND THEIR IMPACT ON REAL-WORLD ACTION

Digital campaigns have become a prominent tool in mobilizing individuals towards real-world actions. These campaigns, facilitated by various online platforms, have the power to reach a vast audience and create significant social impact. By leveraging social media, email marketing, and websites, organizations can disseminate information, raise awareness, and advocate for change on a global scale. The immediacy of digital communication allows for rapid responses to current events, galvanizing supporters to take action in real-time. However, the effectiveness of digital campaigns on real-world action is not without its limitations. The saturation of digital content and the rise of misinformation challenge the credibility and impact of these campaigns. As such, it is crucial for organizations to maintain authenticity, engage with their audience effectively, and strategize how best to convert online engagement into meaningful offline actions. Ultimately, digital campaigns have the potential to drive positive change, but their impact on real-world action hinges on thoughtful planning, execution, and adaptability to the evolving digital landscape.

LII. INTERNET ADDICTION AND THE FUTURE OF HUMAN INTERACTION

The rise of internet addiction poses a significant challenge to the future of human interaction. As individuals become increasingly reliant on technology for social connection, the traditional norms of face-to-face communication are being eroded. This shift has profound implications for society, as interpersonal relationships are fundamentally altered. The prevalence of internet addiction threatens to further isolate individuals, leading to a decline in empathy and emotional connection. Moreover, the constant stimulation provided by online interactions may lead to a decrease in the ability to engage in meaningful real-life conversations. As we navigate this digital landscape, it is crucial to consider the long-term consequences of excessive internet use on human relationships and societal cohesion. Finding a balance between the benefits of technology and the preservation of authentic human connection will be essential in shaping the future of interaction in a digitally-driven world.

THE POTENTIAL FOR ENHANCED COMMUNICATION

The potential for enhanced communication in today's society through technology is undeniable. With the rise of social media platforms, instant messaging apps, and video conferencing tools, individuals can now connect with others from all corners of the globe in real-time. This ease of communication has opened up new avenues for collaboration, networking, and knowledge-sharing. However, this increased connectivity also brings about challenges such as information overload, cyberbullying, and the erosion of face-to-face interactions. As we navigate the double-edged sword of technology, it is essential to strike a balance between leveraging its advantages for improved communication while being mindful of its pitfalls. By being aware of the impact of technology on our communication behaviors, we can harness its potential for enhancing relationships, promoting meaningful dialogue, and fostering a more connected society.

THE RISK OF DIMINISHED FACE-TO-FACE INTERACTIONS

In today's society, the increasing prevalence of internet addiction poses a significant risk of diminished face-to-face interactions among individuals. The allure of constant connectivity and instant gratification through technology has led to a shift away from traditional in-person communication. As individuals become more engrossed in their online personas and virtual interactions, the importance of real-world connections and social skills may be overshadowed. This shift in communication patterns can have wide-reaching implications on interpersonal relationships, emotional intelligence, and overall well-being. Without the nuances of face-to-face interactions, individuals may struggle to develop empathy, understanding, and effective communication skills essential for meaningful relationships. As such, it is crucial to recognize the potential consequences of excessive reliance on technology and take proactive measures to maintain a balance between online and offline interactions in order to preserve the richness and depth of human connection in society.

ADAPTING TO NEW FORMS OF SOCIAL ENGAGEMENT

In adapting to new forms of social engagement in the digital age, individuals must navigate the complexities of online interactions and relationships. The proliferation of social media platforms has revolutionized the way people connect and communicate, presenting both opportunities and challenges. As technology continues to shape social dynamics, individuals need to develop a critical understanding of digital citizenship and online etiquette to foster healthy and meaningful interactions. Striking a balance between virtual and real-world relationships is essential to avoid the pitfalls of internet addiction and social isolation. Furthermore, the ability to adapt to changing norms and behaviors in the digital realm is crucial for maintaining social relevance and relevance in today's society. By embracing the evolving landscape of social engagement, individuals can harness the benefits of technology while mitigating its negative impacts on interpersonal relationships and well-being.

LIII. THE ROLE OF INTERNET ADDICTION IN PERSONAL SAFETY AND SECURITY

The role of internet addiction in personal safety and security is a growing concern in today's society, as individuals become increasingly dependent on online activities. Excessive internet use can lead to a variety of safety risks, including the potential for cyberbullying, online scams, and identity theft. Furthermore, individuals who are addicted to the internet may become more vulnerable to online predators who seek to exploit their vulnerability. It is crucial for policymakers, educators, and parents to address the issue of internet addiction in order to protect individuals from these risks. Implementing measures such as setting limits on screen time, promoting digital literacy, and fostering healthy offline activities can help mitigate the negative impact of internet addiction on personal safety and security. By raising awareness and providing resources for individuals struggling with internet addiction, we can create a safer online environment for all members of society.

ONLINE SCAMS AND PERSONAL VULNERABILITY

Online scams pose a significant threat to individuals' personal financial security and privacy, especially in today's digitally interconnected world. The evolution of technology has made it easier for scammers to lure victims through various deceptive tactics, exploiting individuals' vulnerabilities for financial gain. The rise of online platforms and social media has provided scammers with a wider reach and easier access to potential targets, making it crucial for individuals to be cautious and vigilant when sharing personal information online. Factors such as trust, curiosity, and urgency can increase susceptibility to these scams, highlighting the importance of educating the public about online threats and promoting digital literacy. As technology continues to advance, it is essential for individuals to be aware of the potential risks associated with online activities and take proactive measures to protect themselves from falling victim to online scams.

CYBERSTALKING AND HARASSMENT

Cyberstalking and harassment have become pressing issues in today's digital age, with the anonymity and interconnectedness provided by the internet facilitating such harmful behaviors. The pervasive nature of technology allows perpetrators to target their victims relentlessly, causing significant psychological distress and emotional harm. Cyberstalking often escalates to offline stalking, adding a physical dimension to the threat faced by victims. While laws have been put in place to address cyber harassment, enforcement and prosecution remain challenging due to jurisdictional issues and the difficulty of tracing online perpetrators. Moreover, the impact of cyberstalking extends beyond the individual victims, affecting the larger society by fostering a culture of fear and distrust online. As technology continues to advance, it is imperative for policymakers, law enforcement agencies, and internet platforms to collaborate in developing effective strategies to combat cyberstalking and protect individuals from online harm.

MEASURES FOR ENSURING ONLINE SAFETY

In order to address the issue of internet addiction and its impact on society, measures for ensuring online safety are imperative. One effective strategy is the implementation of parental controls and filters to restrict access to inappropriate content for children and vulnerable individuals. Additionally, promoting digital literacy and responsible online behavior through educational programs and workshops can help individuals navigate the internet more safely. Creating guidelines and regulations for internet usage in schools, workplaces, and public spaces can also play a crucial role in preventing excessive internet use and promoting a healthy balance between online and offline activities. Furthermore, collaboration between governments, tech companies, and mental health professionals is essential in developing comprehensive policies and interventions to combat internet addiction and promote a safer online environment for all users. By implementing these measures, we can mitigate the negative impacts of technology on society and foster a more mindful and balanced relationship with the digital world.

LIV. INTERNET ADDICTION AND THE CONCEPT OF SUCCESS

Internet addiction is a complex phenomenon that has garnered significant attention in recent years due to its detrimental effects on individuals' lives. The concept of success, often associated with achievement, can be distorted when it comes to individuals who are addicted to the internet. Success can be perceived as the number of likes, followers, or views one has online, leading individuals to prioritize virtual validation over real-world accomplishments. This skewed perspective can result in a vicious cycle of seeking validation through online activities, leading to further isolation and disconnection from reality. In a society where success is increasingly measured by online metrics, individuals struggling with internet addiction may find themselves trapped in a downward spiral of comparison and anxiety. It is crucial for researchers and mental health professionals to address the impact of internet addiction on individuals' concepts of success and develop interventions to help them navigate a healthier relationship with technology.

REDEFINING ACHIEVEMENT IN THE DIGITAL AGE

In the digital age, the traditional markers of achievement are being redefined, posing challenges and opportunities for individuals and society as a whole. The widespread adoption of technology has transformed the way we learn, work, and interact, blurring the lines between online and offline accomplishments. As a result, the criteria for success are no longer limited to conventional measures such as academic grades or job titles but encompass a broader range of skills and competencies. In this context, achievement in the digital age involves the ability to adapt to rapid changes, think critically in a sea of information, collaborate effectively in virtual teams, and navigate complex ethical dilemmas. By embracing this new paradigm of achievement, individuals can harness the power of technology to enhance their capabilities and thrive in an increasingly interconnected world. However, this shift also raises concerns about the potential pitfalls of excessive screen time, digital distractions, and the erosion of face-to-face communication skills. As we navigate this evolving landscape, it is crucial to strike a balance between leveraging the benefits of technology and preserving the essential human qualities that define true achievement.

THE PRESSURE OF ONLINE SUCCESS NARRATIVES

The pressure of online success narratives presents a significant challenge in today's society, as individuals are often bombarded with idealized images of achievement and prosperity through social media platforms. This constant exposure to curated narratives of success can create feelings of inadequacy, anxiety, and self-doubt among individuals who compare themselves unfavorably to these seemingly perfect lives. The pressure to conform to these unrealistic standards can lead to an unhealthy obsession with achieving similar levels of success, contributing to the rise of internet addiction. As individuals strive to cultivate their online persona and gain validation through likes and followers, they may neglect real-life relationships and responsibilities, leading to a cycle of isolation and dissatisfaction. It is imperative for researchers to explore the detrimental effects of online success narratives and develop strategies to help individuals navigate these pressures in a healthy and balanced manner.

ALIGNING ONLINE PURSUITS WITH PERSONAL GOALS

In considering the alignment of online pursuits with personal goals, it is crucial to recognize the potential impact on one's well-being and productivity. Technology has made it easier than ever to engage in a wide range of activities online, from social media interactions to academic research. However, individuals must carefully assess how their online activities contribute to or detract from their overall personal goals. For example, spending excessive time on social media platforms may distract individuals from achieving their professional objectives or maintaining healthy relationships. On the other hand, using online resources to further their education or connect with like-minded individuals can be a powerful tool for personal growth. By aligning their online pursuits with their personal goals, individuals can maximize the benefits of technology while minimizing its potentially negative effects on their lives. This thoughtful approach can lead to a more fulfilling and balanced lifestyle in today's digital age.

LV. THE ROLE OF INTERNET ADDICTION IN MENTAL HEALTH AWARENESS

The role of Internet addiction in mental health awareness is a critical aspect that cannot be overlooked in today's society. With the increasing reliance on digital technology, it is essential to understand the potential negative impacts of excessive internet use on mental well-being. Internet addiction has been linked to a range of mental health issues, including anxiety, depression, and social isolation. It is crucial for individuals, especially younger generations, to recognize the signs of internet addiction and seek help when needed. By raising awareness about the detrimental effects of internet addiction, we can promote a healthier relationship with technology and prioritize mental well-being. Through education, counseling, and support services, we can address the root causes of internet addiction and work towards a more balanced and mindful approach to using digital devices. Ultimately, by acknowledging the role of internet addiction in mental health awareness, we can take steps towards a more conscious and proactive society.

ONLINE RESOURCES FOR MENTAL HEALTH SUPPORT

In recent years, the proliferation of online resources for mental health support has been both a blessing and a curse. On one hand, individuals now have unprecedented access to information, support groups, and therapy options at their fingertips. This can be especially beneficial for those who may not have easy access to traditional mental health services due to location, cost, or stigma. However, the abundance of online resources also comes with its own set of challenges. The quality and reliability of information available online can vary widely, leading to confusion and potential harm for vulnerable individuals. Additionally, the anonymity of online interactions can sometimes hinder the development of meaningful therapeutic relationships. Thus, while online resources for mental health support have the potential to greatly benefit individuals, caution must be exercised to ensure that these resources are used effectively and safely in today's society.

THE STIGMA OF MENTAL HEALTH AND ONLINE DISCOURSE

The stigma surrounding mental health is a pervasive issue that has been further exacerbated by online discourse. The anonymity provided by the internet has allowed for harmful stereotypes and misconceptions about mental health to be perpetuated without consequence. Negative attitudes and discrimination towards individuals struggling with mental illnesses are often reinforced in online spaces, leading to further alienation and isolation for those already experiencing mental health challenges. Furthermore, the speed and reach of online communication can amplify these stigmatizing narratives, making it difficult to combat misconceptions and educate the public about the realities of mental health. Addressing the stigma of mental health in online discourse is essential to fostering a more inclusive and understanding society, where individuals feel comfortable seeking help and support without fear of judgment or discrimination.

THE IMPORTANCE OF DIGITAL LITERACY IN MENTAL HEALTH

Digital literacy plays a crucial role in shaping the mental health landscape of individuals in today's society. By understanding how to navigate the vast array of information available online, individuals can access valuable resources and support systems for mental health issues. Digital literacy also enables individuals to discern between credible and unreliable sources of information, reducing the risk of misinformation that can exacerbate mental health conditions. Furthermore, the ability to engage in online communities and platforms allows individuals to connect with others who may be experiencing similar challenges, fostering a sense of belonging and support. As technology continues to advance, the importance of digital literacy in promoting mental well-being cannot be overstated. It is essential for individuals to develop the skills necessary to harness the power of digital tools effectively and responsibly in order to maintain and improve their mental health in today's digital age.

LVI. INTERNET ADDICTION AND THE DYNAMICS OF POWER AND CONTROL

Internet addiction presents a complex interplay of power and control dynamics that contribute to its pervasive nature in today's society. The allure of the internet, with its constant stream of information and connectivity, can create a sense of power for individuals who feel empowered by their access to endless knowledge and communication. However, this very same power can quickly turn into a form of control, as individuals become consumed by the need to constantly engage with online activities and neglect other aspects of their lives. The addictive nature of the internet can perpetuate a cycle of powerlessness and dependence, as individuals struggle to break free from the grip of their online habits. Understanding the dynamics of power and control in internet addiction is essential for developing effective prevention and intervention strategies to address this increasingly prevalent issue.

THE CONCENTRATION OF POWER IN TECH COMPANIES

The concentration of power in tech companies has raised concerns about monopolistic practices and the immense influence these firms hold over various aspects of society. With major players like Google, Facebook, Amazon, and Apple dominating the market, there is a growing need for regulatory measures to prevent these companies from abusing their power. The accumulation of vast amounts of data by these tech giants also poses a threat to user privacy and data security, further exacerbating the issue. Moreover, the potential for these companies to stifle competition and innovation raises questions about the long-term implications for consumers and the economy. As these tech companies continue to expand their reach and influence, it becomes imperative for policymakers to address the concentration of power in the tech industry to ensure a fair and competitive marketplace for all stakeholders involved.

USER AUTONOMY AND CONTROL OVER ONLINE EXPERIENCES

User autonomy and control over online experiences play a crucial role in understanding the phenomenon of internet addiction. Users who have a strong sense of control over their online behaviors are less likely to develop addictive tendencies. This autonomy allows individuals to make informed decisions about their online activities and set boundaries for themselves. However, in today's society, the line between autonomy and addiction is becoming increasingly blurred. The constant stream of notifications, social pressures, and personalized content algorithms can easily overwhelm users and erode their sense of control. As a result, many individuals find themselves compulsively checking their devices, seeking validation from social media, and sacrificing real-world relationships for digital gratification. It is essential for researchers to delve deeper into how users navigate the online world, identify the factors that influence their autonomy, and develop strategies to promote healthy online behaviors.

THE BALANCE OF POWER IN THE DIGITAL ECOSYSTEM

The balance of power in the digital ecosystem is a crucial aspect to consider in understanding the complexities of internet addiction and its impact on today's society. With the rapid advancement of technology, various stakeholders such as governments, corporations, and individuals are constantly vying for control and influence within this interconnected web of information. Power dynamics can manifest in the form of data ownership, regulatory frameworks, and online behavior monitoring, shaping the way individuals interact with digital platforms. By examining the distribution of power in the digital space, we can uncover how certain entities may exploit vulnerabilities for their own gain, leading to detrimental consequences like the proliferation of addiction and manipulation of user behavior. Understanding and navigating the intricate balance of power in the digital ecosystem is essential for mitigating the negative effects of internet addiction and promoting a healthier online society.

LVII. THE ROLE OF INTERNET ADDICTION IN GLOBALIZATION

The role of internet addiction in globalization, a complex phenomenon that intertwines technology and society, is a significant topic of interest in today's digital world. As individuals become increasingly dependent on the internet for communication, information, and entertainment, the lines between virtual and reality blur. This addiction not only affects personal mental health and well-being but also has broader implications for social interactions and cultural practices on a global scale. The constant access to online platforms can lead to a detachment from the physical world, impacting how individuals engage with their surroundings and relationships. Furthermore, the spread of internet addiction can contribute to the homogenization of cultures and values, as people become more connected through virtual spaces than physical communities. Understanding the impact of internet addiction in the context of globalization is crucial for addressing the challenges and potential risks posed by this technological revolution.

THE INTERNET AS A TOOL FOR CROSS-BORDER COMMUNICATION

The Internet has become an indispensable tool for cross-border communication, facilitating interactions between individuals, businesses, and governments across the globe. With the advancement of technology, the internet has made it easier for people to connect and communicate with others from different cultural backgrounds, languages, and geographical locations. This connectivity has led to an increase in international collaboration, knowledge sharing, and cultural exchange, bridging the gaps that once hindered effective communication. However, the internet also presents challenges in terms of privacy, security, and information accuracy, which can impact the quality and reliability of cross-border communication. As we delve deeper into the impact of the internet on society, it is essential to explore both the benefits and limitations of this powerful tool in order to maximize its potential for fostering meaningful and productive cross-border communication in today's interconnected world.

THE IMPACT ON CULTURAL EXCHANGE AND UNDERSTANDING

The impact of technology on cultural exchange and understanding in today's society is profound and multifaceted. On one hand, the internet has facilitated unprecedented connectivity between individuals from different cultural backgrounds, allowing for the exchange of ideas, customs, and traditions on a global scale. This has the potential to foster cross-cultural understanding and empathy, ultimately contributing to a more tolerant and inclusive society. However, on the other hand, the digital age has also led to the proliferation of echo chambers and the reinforcement of cultural stereotypes, creating barriers to genuine intercultural communication. As individuals become more immersed in their online communities, they may inadvertently isolate themselves from opposing viewpoints, hindering their ability to engage in meaningful dialogue with those who hold different beliefs. Thus, while technology has the power to bridge cultural divides, it is essential for individuals to approach digital interactions with awareness and critical thinking in order to truly harness its potential for promoting cross-cultural understanding.

THE CHALLENGES OF GLOBAL CONNECTIVITY

The challenges of global connectivity are vast and multifaceted, posing significant obstacles to individuals, societies, and nations alike. As technology continues to advance at a rapid pace, the world becomes increasingly interconnected, blurring the boundaries between physical and digital realms. This interconnectedness brings with it a host of challenges, from cybersecurity threats and data privacy concerns to the spread of misinformation and the erosion of traditional social structures. The reliance on digital communication and virtual platforms has also given rise to issues such as internet addiction, social isolation, and the commodification of personal data. These challenges require a nuanced and multifaceted approach, combining technological solutions with policy interventions and societal changes to navigate the complex landscape of global connectivity. As we strive to harness the benefits of technology while minimizing its negative impacts, it is essential to critically examine the challenges posed by global connectivity and work towards sustainable solutions for a more connected world.

LVIII. INTERNET ADDICTION AND THE SHIFTING NATURE OF KNOWLEDGE

The rise of internet addiction in today's society has sparked concerns about the shifting nature of knowledge acquisition. With the constant barrage of information available online, individuals may find themselves overwhelmed by the sheer volume of data at their fingertips. This phenomenon raises questions about the quality and reliability of the knowledge being consumed, as well as the impact on critical thinking skills and cognitive processing. As individuals become more reliant on the internet for information, there is a risk of a decline in the ability to engage in deep, analytical thinking and discernment of credible sources. It is crucial for researchers and educators to address this issue and promote a balanced approach to information consumption that encourages thoughtful analysis and evaluation. By acknowledging the potential pitfalls of internet addiction, society can work towards harnessing the benefits of technology while safeguarding against its negative consequences.

THE ACCESSIBILITY OF INFORMATION ONLINE

The accessibility of information online has revolutionized the way we gather and disseminate knowledge in today's society. With just a few clicks, individuals can access a vast amount of information on virtually any topic, making research and learning more convenient and efficient. This ease of access has paved the way for increased collaboration, innovation, and connectivity among individuals across the globe. However, the abundance of information online also poses challenges, such as the difficulty in discerning credible sources from misinformation or the overwhelming amount of data that can lead to information overload. As technology continues to evolve, it is essential for individuals to develop critical thinking skills to navigate the vast sea of information available online effectively. By striking a balance between accessibility and discernment, we can harness the power of online information while mitigating the potential negative consequences associated with it.

THE QUESTION OF KNOWLEDGE OWNERSHIP

One of the key issues surrounding internet addiction is the question of knowledge ownership. As individuals spend more time online, they are constantly consuming information from various sources, but the question arises as to who owns this knowledge. With the ease of access to information on the internet, it becomes challenging to trace the origins of ideas and concepts, leading to debates about intellectual property rights and plagiarism. This issue is further compounded by the interconnected nature of the online world, where ideas are shared and circulated rapidly. As such, it is imperative for society to establish clear guidelines and regulations to address the ownership of knowledge in the digital age. By acknowledging and respecting the ownership of knowledge, we can foster a culture of accountability and integrity in online interactions, ultimately mitigating the negative impacts of internet addiction on society.

THE ROLE OF CRITICAL THINKING IN THE INFORMATION AGE

In the Information Age, the ability to think critically is more crucial than ever before. With the overwhelming flood of information available at our fingertips, individuals must possess the skills to evaluate, analyze, and synthesize this data to make informed decisions. Critical thinking allows individuals to question sources, identify biases, and discern fact from opinion in a world where misinformation and fake news abound. In the realm of internet addiction, critical thinking serves as a powerful tool to combat the negative impacts of excessive technology use. By engaging in critical reflection on the usage patterns and psychological effects of technology, individuals can take proactive steps to mitigate the risks of addiction and maintain a healthy balance in their lives. Ultimately, the cultivation of critical thinking skills is essential in navigating the complexities of the Information Age and fostering a more discerning and informed society.

LIX. THE ROLE OF INTERNET ADDICTION IN SHAPING FUTURE GENERATIONS

The role of internet addiction in shaping future generations is a critical issue that requires careful examination. As the prevalence of technology continues to increase, especially among younger demographics, the impact of excessive internet use on individuals' cognitive, emotional, and social development cannot be understated. Research has shown that prolonged exposure to online activities can lead to a decline in academic performance, increased levels of anxiety and depression, and weakened interpersonal relationships. Therefore, it is imperative for society to address the potential consequences of internet addiction on the upcoming generations. By developing effective prevention strategies, promoting healthy digital habits, and providing support for those affected by internet addiction, we can strive to create a more balanced and sustainable relationship with technology for the future. As technology continues to evolve, it is crucial to consider the long-term implications of internet addiction on the well-being of individuals and society as a whole.

THE DIGITAL NATIVE PHENOMENON

The digital native phenomenon, characterized by individuals who have grown up in a digital environment, has become a prominent subject of study in recent years. These individuals, often referred to as Generation Z, have been exposed to technology from a young age, leading to a high level of comfort and proficiency in using digital devices and platforms. While this fluency can be advantageous in terms of accessing information and engaging with others online, it has also been linked to concerns such as internet addiction. Excessive use of technology can lead to detrimental effects on mental health, social skills, and productivity. As society becomes increasingly reliant on technology, it is crucial to understand the double-edged sword of the digital native phenomenon, acknowledging both its benefits and potential drawbacks. By recognizing the impact of technology on today's society, we can work towards finding a balance that harnesses the advantages of digital proficiency while minimizing the risks associated with internet addiction.

PREPARING YOUTH FOR A DIGITAL FUTURE

Preparing youth for a digital future is a multifaceted task that requires a comprehensive approach to education and training. In order to equip young individuals with the skills and knowledge needed to thrive in an increasingly digital society, it is essential for schools and educational institutions to incorporate computer science and digital literacy into their curriculum. This can include teaching coding, software development, and digital citizenship to help young people navigate the online world responsibly. Beyond technical skills, it is important to emphasize critical thinking, problem-solving, and adaptability, as these qualities are crucial for success in a rapidly evolving digital landscape. By empowering youth with the tools they need to effectively engage with technology, we can ensure that they are prepared to harness its potential for innovation and progress, while also mitigating the risks associated with excessive screen time and internet addiction.

THE RESPONSIBILITY OF GUIDING RESPONSIBLE INTERNET USE

One of the key components in addressing internet addiction and its impact on society is the responsibility of guiding responsible internet use. This involves not only educating individuals on the potential risks of excessive internet use but also providing them with the tools and resources necessary to navigate the online world in a healthy manner. Parents, educators, and policymakers all play crucial roles in promoting responsible internet use, whether through setting limits on screen time, teaching digital literacy skills, or advocating for regulations that protect users from harmful online content. By emphasizing the importance of balance, critical thinking, and mindfulness in online activities, we can help individuals develop a healthy relationship with technology and reduce the negative consequences associated with internet addiction. Ultimately, guiding responsible internet use is essential in creating a society that thrives in the digital age without succumbing to its drawbacks.

LX. INTERNET ADDICTION AND THE CONCEPT OF LEISURE

Internet addiction has become a growing concern in today's society, with individuals spending an increasing amount of time online, often at the expense of traditional leisure activities. This shift raises questions about the evolving nature of leisure in the digital age. While some argue that time spent on the internet can be a form of leisure, others argue that true leisure involves active participation and engagement with the physical world. This discrepancy highlights the need to reevaluate our understanding of leisure in the context of technology. The allure of constant connectivity and instant gratification provided by the internet can lead individuals to prioritize online activities over more meaningful forms of leisure, potentially hindering personal development and overall well-being. As such, further research is needed to explore the implications of internet addiction on how we perceive and engage in leisure activities in the modern world.

THE TRANSFORMATION OF LEISURE ACTIVITIES

The transformation of leisure activities in today's society has been greatly impacted by the advancement of technology, particularly the widespread use of the internet. Traditional forms of leisure, such as reading a book or playing outside, have been increasingly replaced by screen-based activities like social media browsing, online gaming, and streaming services. This shift has raised concerns about the potential negative effects of internet addiction on individuals' mental and physical health. Despite the convenience and entertainment value that technology provides, it is crucial to examine the consequences of excessive screen time on personal well-being. Understanding how leisure activities have evolved in the digital age can help researchers and policymakers develop interventions to promote a balanced lifestyle and mitigate the detrimental effects of internet addiction on society as a whole.

THE ROLE OF THE INTERNET IN RELAXATION AND DOWNTIME

The internet plays a significant role in providing relaxation and downtime for individuals in today's society. With the vast array of entertainment options available online, such as streaming services, social media platforms, and online gaming, people can easily unwind and escape from the stresses of daily life. Engaging in these online activities can offer a sense of enjoyment and distraction, allowing individuals to temporarily disconnect from their responsibilities and obligations. Additionally, the internet offers a virtual space for socialization and interaction, enabling people to connect with others and form relationships from the comfort of their own homes. However, it is essential to recognize the potential downside of excessive internet use, as it can lead to addiction and negative consequences for mental health and well-being. Therefore, while the internet can be a valuable tool for relaxation and leisure, moderation and mindfulness are crucial in maintaining a healthy balance in the digital age.

FINDING LEISURE BEYOND THE SCREEN

Finding leisure beyond the screen has become increasingly important in today's society dominated by technology. As individuals spend more time on their devices, there is a growing need to find alternative ways to relax and unwind. This shift away from screens can lead to improved mental health and overall well-being. Engaging in physical activities such as hiking, yoga, or simply taking a walk in nature can provide a much-needed break from the constant stimulation of screens. Additionally, socializing with friends and family face-to-face or participating in community events can foster meaningful connections and create a sense of belonging. By finding leisure activities beyond the screen, individuals can reduce their reliance on technology and achieve a better balance in their lives. This shift can ultimately lead to a healthier lifestyle and a more fulfilling sense of leisure.

LXI. THE ROLE OF INTERNET ADDICTION IN THE ARTS AND CULTURE

The role of internet addiction in the arts and culture is a complex and multifaceted issue that warrants careful examination. As technology continues to evolve at a rapid pace, the ways in which individuals engage with and consume artistic content have also transformed. Internet addiction can lead to a range of detrimental effects on artistic practices and cultural experiences, such as reduced attention spans, altered perceptions of creativity, and a shift towards instant gratification. However, it is important to acknowledge that the internet also offers unprecedented opportunities for artists and cultural producers to reach new audiences and experiment with innovative forms of expression. By critically analyzing the interplay between internet addiction and the arts, researchers can develop a more nuanced understanding of the digital landscape and its implications for contemporary culture. Ultimately, striking a balance between harnessing the benefits of digital technology while mitigating its potential harms is key to fostering a vibrant and sustainable artistic ecosystem in the digital age.

DIGITAL ART AND ONLINE EXHIBITIONS

Digital art and online exhibitions have become increasingly prevalent in today's society, offering new avenues for artists to showcase their work and for audiences to engage with art from anywhere in the world. The accessibility and convenience of online platforms have democratized the art world, allowing emerging artists to reach a global audience and challenging traditional notions of curation and display. However, this shift to the digital realm also raises questions about the authenticity and value of art in a virtual space. Critics argue that the physicality and sensory experiences tied to traditional galleries are lost in online exhibitions, impacting the viewer's emotional connection to the artwork. As technology continues to advance, the debate between the merits of digital art and the importance of physical interaction in art consumption will remain at the forefront of discussions surrounding the evolving landscape of the art world.

THE PRESERVATION OF CULTURAL ARTIFACTS

The preservation of cultural artifacts is of paramount importance in today's society, as these objects hold immense historical, artistic, and cultural significance. With the rise of technology, there are now innovative ways to digitize and protect these valuable artifacts from the natural wear and tear of time. Museums and institutions can now use advanced imaging techniques to create virtual replicas of ancient artifacts, allowing people from all over the world to access and appreciate these treasures. However, while technology offers new possibilities for preservation, there are also challenges that come with it. The ever-evolving nature of digital platforms means that we must continuously update and maintain these virtual collections to ensure their longevity. Despite these challenges, the digital preservation of cultural artifacts presents a promising solution to safeguarding our rich heritage for future generations to appreciate and learn from.

THE INFLUENCE OF DIGITAL MEDIA ON ARTISTIC EXPRESSION

The influence of digital media on artistic expression is a topic of great interest in contemporary society. The advent of technology has provided artists with a myriad of creative tools and platforms to showcase their work to a global audience. Through social media, websites, and digital galleries, artists can reach a wider audience and engage with their viewers in new and innovative ways. Digital media has also democratized the art world, allowing emerging artists to showcase their work alongside established professionals. However, some argue that the ubiquity of digital media has led to a homogenization of artistic expression, with trends and styles easily propagated and replicated. Despite these concerns, digital media continues to shape and redefine the boundaries of artistic practice, challenging artists to push the limits of creativity and experimentation in the digital age.

LXII. INTERNET ADDICTION AND THE NOTION OF COMMUNITY SERVICE

Internet addiction has become a prevalent issue in today's society, with individuals spending excessive amounts of time online, neglecting real-life relationships and responsibilities. However, it is crucial to consider the potential positive impact of internet use, particularly in the context of community service. Online platforms provide a unique opportunity for individuals to engage in volunteer work, raise awareness about social issues, and connect with like-minded individuals who share a passion for giving back to their communities. By harnessing the power of the internet for community service, individuals suffering from internet addiction can channel their energy into meaningful and productive activities that benefit society as a whole. Furthermore, fostering a sense of online community can help combat feelings of isolation and disconnection that often contribute to addictive behaviors. Overall, exploring the intersection of internet addiction and community service can shed light on the complex relationship between technology and social responsibility in the digital age.

ONLINE VOLUNTEERING AND SOCIAL IMPACT

Online volunteering has become an increasingly popular method through which individuals can contribute to social impact initiatives. By harnessing the power of the internet, volunteers can participate in projects and causes from anywhere in the world, expanding the reach and effectiveness of their efforts. From providing remote tutoring to underserved communities to helping organizations with graphic design work, online volunteering offers a diverse range of opportunities for individuals to make a difference. However, while the convenience and accessibility of online volunteering are undeniable, it is essential to consider the potential drawbacks and limitations of this approach. Issues such as digital divide, accountability, and the quality of work produced remotely must be carefully evaluated to ensure that online volunteering truly achieves meaningful social impact. As technology continues to advance, it is crucial for researchers and practitioners to critically assess the implications of online volunteering on society and develop strategies to maximize its benefits while mitigating potential risks.

THE ROLE OF THE INTERNET IN MOBILIZING AID

The role of the Internet in mobilizing aid has become increasingly significant in modern society. Through online platforms and social media, individuals can quickly and efficiently organize support for various causes and disasters. The internet enables rapid communication, fundraising, and coordination of resources on a global scale, allowing for more effective and immediate responses to crises. However, the prevalence of fake news and misinformation online poses a challenge in ensuring the accuracy and legitimacy of aid efforts. It is crucial for aid organizations and individuals to verify the credibility of information before taking action. As technology continues to advance, the internet's role in mobilizing aid will only grow, emphasizing the need for critical thinking and discernment in leveraging online resources for humanitarian purposes.

THE ETHICS OF DIGITAL HUMANITARIANISM

The ethics of digital humanitarianism lie at the intersection of technology, morality, and social responsibility. As the digital landscape continues to evolve and expand, the potential for leveraging technology for humanitarian purposes becomes increasingly apparent. However, this also raises ethical questions about the appropriate use of digital tools in humanitarian efforts. On one hand, technology can enable more efficient disaster response, facilitate communication and coordination among aid organizations, and amplify the voices of marginalized communities. Yet, on the other hand, concerns about data privacy, surveillance, and the digital divide must be carefully weighed. It is crucial for researchers, policymakers, and practitioners to critically assess the ethical implications of digital humanitarianism, considering issues such as consent, transparency, accountability, and equity. By approaching digital humanitarianism with a thoughtful and ethical lens, we can harness the power of technology while safeguarding the rights and dignity of those in need.

LXIII. THE ROLE OF INTERNET ADDICTION IN PERSONAL BRANDING

In today's digital age, the concept of personal branding has become increasingly important in various aspects of life, including professional success, social relationships, and self-image. However, the rise of internet addiction poses a significant challenge to individuals seeking to cultivate a strong personal brand. Internet addiction can lead to excessive time spent online, which may detract from the individual's ability to engage in meaningful self-reflection, pursue personal growth opportunities, or build authentic connections with others. Moreover, the constant bombardment of information and social media platforms can distort one's self-perception and overshadow their unique qualities and talents. Therefore, it is crucial for individuals to strike a balance between utilizing the internet for personal branding purposes and maintaining a healthy relationship with technology to avoid the detrimental effects of internet addiction on their personal brand. By acknowledging the role of internet addiction in personal branding and implementing strategies to manage online behavior, individuals can enhance their image and reputation in a mindful and sustainable manner.

THE RISE OF THE INFLUENCER CULTURE

The rise of the influencer culture in today's society is a phenomenon that cannot be ignored. Influencers, often leveraging social media platforms, have amassed massive followings and wield significant influence over their audiences. This newfound power has led to collaborations with brands, shaping consumer behavior and trends. However, the influencer culture also brings to light ethical concerns, such as authenticity and the promotion of materialism. The constant exposure to curated images and lifestyles may contribute to feelings of inadequacy and perpetuate unrealistic standards. As technology continues to advance, the influencer culture raises questions about the impact of social media on mental health and self-esteem. It is essential for researchers to delve deeper into the complexities of this cultural shift to understand its implications on today's society fully.

MANAGING ONLINE REPUTATION

Managing online reputation is a crucial aspect in today's digital age, where individuals and businesses are vulnerable to the instantaneous spread of information online. In order to navigate the complex landscape of the internet, it is essential for entities to proactively monitor their online presence and address any negative content promptly. Utilizing various online tools such as social media monitoring platforms and search engine optimization techniques can help in maintaining a positive reputation. Additionally, engaging with customers and stakeholders through transparent communication and actively seeking feedback can contribute to a favorable online image. By prioritizing reputation management strategies, individuals and organizations can mitigate potential risks and cultivate a strong online presence in an increasingly interconnected world. The ability to effectively manage online reputation is paramount in safeguarding credibility and trust in today's society dominated by digital interactions.

THE IMPACT OF PERSONAL BRANDING ON CAREER OPPORTUNITIES

Personal branding plays a crucial role in shaping career opportunities in today's competitive job market. Individuals who effectively cultivate and manage their personal brand are more likely to stand out among their peers and attract attention from potential employers. By strategically showcasing their skills, expertise, and unique qualities online through social media platforms, personal websites, and networking events, individuals can position themselves as desirable candidates for job opportunities. A strong personal brand can help individuals establish credibility, build trust with prospective employers, and differentiate themselves from others with similar qualifications. Moreover, a well-defined personal brand can open doors to new career opportunities, expand professional networks, and ultimately lead to career advancement. In essence, investing time and effort in developing a personal brand can significantly enhance an individual's career prospects and create new avenues for success in the professional world.

LXIV. INTERNET ADDICTION AND THE EVOLUTION OF HUMAN CONSCIOUSNESS

Internet addiction has become a pressing issue in today's society, with individuals increasingly dependent on digital devices for communication, information, and entertainment. This phenomenon raises questions about how the evolution of human consciousness is being shaped by constant online connectivity. The internet's vast array of information and immediate gratification has the potential to alter the way individuals think, process information, and interact with the world around them. As individuals spend more time online, their brains may become rewired to prioritize digital stimuli over real-life experiences. This shift in cognitive processes could have profound implications for how humans perceive reality, form relationships, and make decisions. Therefore, examining the relationship between internet addiction and the evolution of human consciousness is crucial for understanding the complex interplay between technology and cognitive development in the modern age.

THE INFLUENCE ON COGNITIVE PROCESSES

The influence of technology on cognitive processes is a complex and multifaceted issue that deserves thorough examination. One key aspect to consider is the impact of technology, particularly the internet, on attention span and concentration. Research has shown that excessive use of the internet can lead to decreased cognitive control and increased distractibility. This can have wide-reaching implications for individuals' ability to focus, problem-solve, and engage in critical thinking tasks. Moreover, the constant stimuli and notifications from digital devices can overwhelm the brain's cognitive processes, leading to information overload and reduced cognitive efficiency. Understanding these effects is crucial in order to develop effective strategies to mitigate the negative consequences of internet addiction and promote healthy cognitive functioning in today's society. By exploring these issues in depth, we can gain valuable insights into the ways in which technology shapes our cognitive processes and ultimately influences our behavior and well-being.

THE POTENTIAL FOR EXPANDING AWARENESS

The potential for expanding awareness of the detrimental effects of internet addiction on today's society is crucial for addressing this pressing issue. By increasing awareness, individuals, families, educators, and policymakers can better understand the impact of excessive internet use on mental health, relationships, and overall well-being. Education and public awareness campaigns can help to highlight the warning signs of internet addiction and provide resources for those seeking help. Additionally, research efforts focused on the prevalence of internet addiction and its consequences can contribute to a deeper understanding of this phenomenon. Through collaboration between researchers, healthcare professionals, and technology companies, innovative solutions and interventions can be developed to mitigate the negative effects of internet addiction. By expanding awareness and fostering interdisciplinary collaboration, society can work towards creating a healthier relationship with technology.

THE INTERSECTION OF TECHNOLOGY AND SPIRITUALITY

The intersection of technology and spirituality is a complex and dynamic area that has gained increasing attention in recent years. On one hand, technology has provided tools and platforms for individuals to engage with their spirituality in new and innovative ways, such as through meditation apps, virtual religious services, and online communities for spiritual exploration. These technological advancements have facilitated greater access to spiritual practices and teachings, breaking down barriers of time and space. On the other hand, there are concerns about the potential negative impact of technology on spirituality, as it can lead to distractions, disconnection from the physical world, and a shallow engagement with spiritual practices. As researchers continue to explore this intersection, it is crucial to examine both the positive and negative implications of technology on spirituality, and to develop strategies for harnessing technology in ways that enhance, rather than detract from, spiritual growth and well-being in today's society.

LXV. CONCLUSION

In conclusion, the prevalence of internet addiction in modern society is a complex issue that requires further research and attention. The double sides of technology, with its countless benefits and drawbacks, have created a new challenge for individuals and communities worldwide. As discussed in this essay, internet addiction can have significant impacts on individuals' mental health, relationships, and productivity. Understanding the factors contributing to internet addiction and developing effective interventions is crucial to addressing this growing problem. It is imperative for policymakers, healthcare professionals, and technology companies to collaborate in implementing strategies that promote healthier internet use and reduce the negative consequences of excessive screen time. By raising awareness and fostering a comprehensive approach to combating internet addiction, we can strive towards a more balanced and sustainable relationship with technology in today's society.

SUMMARY OF KEY FINDINGS

In summary, the key findings of this research highlight the detrimental effects of internet addiction on today's society. The prevalence of this issue has been shown to lead to various negative consequences, such as decreased productivity, social isolation, and potential mental health problems. Furthermore, the accessibility and constant connectivity provided by technology have contributed to the rise of internet addiction, making it a growing concern among individuals of all ages. Additionally, the impact of internet addiction extends beyond the individual, affecting relationships, work performance, and overall well-being. It is evident that more awareness and research are needed to address this issue effectively and develop strategies to mitigate its effects on society. Overall, the findings underscore the urgency of addressing internet addiction as a serious societal concern that requires attention and intervention.

IMPLICATIONS FOR FUTURE RESEARCH

Implications for future research in the field of internet addiction and its impact on today's society are vast and critical. One avenue for further exploration could be to delve into the underlying psychological mechanisms that drive individuals to develop addictive behaviors towards technology. Understanding the cognitive processes involved in internet addiction could lead to more targeted interventions and prevention strategies. Additionally, longitudinal studies could shed light on the long-term consequences of internet addiction on individuals' mental health, relationships, and overall well-being. Another fruitful area for future research could be to examine the role of societal factors, such as cultural norms and economic conditions, in shaping patterns of internet use and addiction. By exploring these various dimensions, researchers can contribute to a more comprehensive understanding of the complex phenomenon of internet addiction and its implications for society at large.

FINAL THOUGHTS ON THE DOUBLE SIDES OF TECHNOLOGY

In conclusion, the double sides of technology, particularly the phenomenon of internet addiction, present a complex and multifaceted issue that requires careful consideration and intervention. While technology has undoubtedly revolutionized the way we live, work, and communicate, it also brings with it a host of negative consequences, such as increased screen time, social isolation, and diminished mental health. As our society becomes more reliant on technology, it is imperative that we address these challenges head-on through a combination of education, regulation, and personal responsibility. By fostering a greater awareness of the risks associated with technology use and promoting healthy habits and boundaries, we can mitigate the harmful effects of internet addiction and create a more balanced and sustainable relationship with technology in today's society. Only by recognizing and addressing the double sides of technology can we harness its benefits while minimizing its drawbacks.

BIBLIOGRAPHY

Janice Reynolds. 'Logistics and Fulfillment for e-business.' A Practical Guide to Mastering Back Office Functions for Online Commerce, CRC Press, 4/15/2001

Alan Booth. 'Children's Influence on Family Dynamics.' The Neglected Side of Family Relationships, Ann C. Crouter, Routledge, 4/2/2003

Markie L. C. Blumer. 'The Couple and Family Technology Framework.' Intimate Relationships in a Digital Age, Katherine M. Hertlein, Routledge, 7/18/2013

Amir H. Pakpour. 'A Good Sleep: The Role of Factors in Psychosocial Health.' Chung-Ying Lin, Frontiers Media SA, 7/8/2020

David B. Cooper. 'Introduction to Mental Health.' Substance Use, CRC Press, 11/22/2017

Ahmad Alkhatib. 'Sedentary Lifestyle.' Predictive Factors, Health Risks and Physiological Implications, Nova Science Publishers, Incorporated, 1/1/2016

Olatz Lopez-Fernandez. 'Internet and Smartphone Use-Related Addiction Health Problems.' Treatment, Education and Research, MDPI, 8/31/2021

Robert C. Carlson. 'Personal Finance After 50 For Dummies.' Eric Tyson, John Wiley & Sons, 8/7/2018

Thomas H. Davenport. 'The Attention Economy.' Understanding the New Currency of Business, Harvard Business School Press, 1/1/2001

Cary Cooper. 'Healthy and Productive Work.' An International Perspective, Lawrence R. Murphy, CRC Press, 6/29/2000

Martin Reuter. 'Internet Addiction.' Neuroscientific Approaches and Therapeutical Implications Including Smartphone Addiction, Christian Montag, Springer International Publishing, 5/8/2018

Nancy J. Allen. 'Toward Digital Equity.' Bridging the Divide in Education, Gwen Solomon, Allyn and Bacon, 1/1/2003

DIWAKAR EDUCATION HUB.'CUET-PG Philosophy [HUQP16] Question Bank Book 3000+ Question Answer Chapter Wise As Per Updated Syllabus.' Diwakar Education Hub , 2/1/2024

Kumar, A.V. Senthil. 'Optimizing Student Engagement in Online Learning Environments.' IGI Global, 11/30/2017

C. David Hollister. 'Distance Learning.' Principles for Effective Design, Delivery, and Evaluation, Chandra Mehrotra, SAGE Publications, 9/21/2001

Dr. C. Swarnalatha. 'A HANDBOOK ON WORK-LIFE BALANCE.' Lulu.com, 1/12/2017

Productive Luddite. 'Focuscrime: Maxims and Mantras for Recovering Multitaskers and the Desperately Distracted.' The Productive Luddite, 6/1/2010

Doug Knell. 'Innovative Internet Secrets.' Increase your internet productivity and efficiency by a factor of ten or more, Innovasion, 1/11/2018

Michael Ball. 'E-Management @ Work.' The Internet and the Office Productivity Revolution, Godefroy Beauvallet, iUniverse, 1/1/2002

Barry Schwartz. 'The Paradox of Choice.' Why More Is Less, Revised Edition, Harper Collins, 10/13/2009

Batista, Joao Carlos Lopes. 'Information and Communication Overload in the Digital Age.' Marques, Rui Pedro Figueiredo, IGI Global, 1/30/2017

Jeffrey Huber. 'HIV/AIDS Internet Information Sources and Resources.' CRC Press, 4/29/2021

Juan Manuel Machimbarrena. 'Risks of "Cyber-relationships" in Adolescents and Young People.' Iratxe Redondo, Frontiers Media SA, 2/17/2023

Palanichamy Naveen. 'Understanding the Metaverse and its Technological Marvels.' Beyond Reality, Cambridge Scholars Publishing, 12/11/2023

Burrow-Sanchez, Jason. 'Adolescent Online Social Communication and Behavior: Relationship Formation on the Internet.' Relationship Formation on the Internet, Zheng, Robert Z., IGI Global, 11/30/2009

274

Adrian Carr. 'Cyberspace Romance.' The Psychology of Online Relationships, Monica Whitty, Bloomsbury Publishing, 9/16/2017

Paul Delfabbro. 'Internet Gaming Disorder.' Theory, Assessment, Treatment, and Prevention, Daniel King, Academic Press, 7/18/2018

Richard M. Ryan. 'Glued to Games.' How Video Games Draw Us In and Hold Us Spellbound, Scott Rigby, Bloomsbury Publishing USA, 2/18/2011

Richard A. Bartle. 'MMOs from the Inside Out.' The History, Design, Fun, and Art of Massively-multiplayer Online Role-playing Games, Apress, 12/30/2015

Sarah Gentry. 'Internet Addiction and Online Gaming.' Samuel C. McQuade, Chelsea House, 1/1/2012

Juliette Powell. 'Social Media Feedback Loops.' Pearson Education Incorporated, 1/1/1900

Gabriele Meiselwitz. 'Social Computing and Social Media. Design, Ethics, User Behavior, and Social Network Analysis.' 12th International Conference, SCSM 2020, Held as Part of the 22nd HCI International Conference, HCII 2020, Copenhagen, Denmark, July 19–24, 2020, Proceedings, Part I, Springer Nature, 7/10/2020

John Allen Hendricks. 'Social Media.' Usage and Impact, Hana S. Noor Al-Deen, Lexington Books, 1/1/2012

Andrea C. Nakaya. 'Internet and Social Media Addiction.' ReferencePoint Press, Incorporated ®, 1/1/2015

Shazib Naveed. 'Internet Usage & Task Preferences Part 1.' A Perspective with Gender Differences, Lap Lambert Academic Publishing GmbH KG, 1/1/2013

Division of Behavioral and Social Sciences and Education. 'Ending Discrimination Against People with Mental and Substance Use Disorders.' The Evidence for Stigma Change, National Academies of Sciences, Engineering, and Medicine, National Academies Press, 9/3/2016

Division of Behavioral and Social Sciences and Education. 'High and Rising Mortality Rates Among Working-Age Adults.' National Academies of Sciences, Engineering, and Medicine, National Academies Press, 1/1/2021

Jindal, Priya. 'Promoting Consumer Engagement Through Emotional Branding and Sensory Marketing.' Gupta, Monika, IGI Global, 12/9/2022

I. Albery. 'Cognition and Addiction.' Marcus Munafò, Oxford University Press, 1/1/2006

Bozoglan, Bahadir. 'Psychological, Social, and Cultural Aspects of Internet Addiction.' IGI Global, 12/8/2017

Bonnie A. Nardi. 'Materiality and Organizing.' Social Interaction in a Technological World, Paul M. Leonardi, OUP Oxford, 11/22/2012

Johnny Ryan. 'A History of the Internet and the Digital Future.' Reaktion Books, 9/15/2010

Paolo Magaudda. 'A History of Digital Media.' An Intermedia and Global Perspective, Gabriele Balbi, Routledge, 4/24/2018

Meryl Siegal. 'Generation 1.5 in College Composition.' Teaching Academic Writing to U.S.-Educated Learners of ESL, Mark Roberge, Routledge, 2/12/2009

Cristiano Nabuco de Abreu. 'Internet Addiction.' A Handbook and Guide to Evaluation and Treatment, Kimberly S. Young, Wiley, 10/26/2010

Laura Curtiss Feder PsyD. 'Behavioral Addictions.' Criteria, Evidence, and Treatment, Kenneth Paul Rosenberg MD, Academic Press, 2/17/2014

Cristiano Nabuco De Abreu, PhD. 'Internet Addiction in Children and Adolescents.' Risk Factors, Assessment, and Treatment, Kimberly S. Young, PsyD, Springer Publishing Company, 6/28/2017